INSIGHT POCKET GUIDE

Bahamas

APA PUBLICATIONS
Part of the Langenscheidt Publishing Group

New Providence

2 miles / 3 km

Northeast Providence Channel

Hanover Sound

White Bank

Salt Cay

Paradise Isl. Golf Course
CABBAGE BEACH
Paradise Isl. The Narrows
CABBAGE BEACH
MONTAGU BEACH
Athol Island

Sea Gardens
Fort Montagu
Dick's Point
Yacht Haven
Peel Deck

East End Point
Camperdown
Blackbeard's Tower
Creek Village
Culberts Point
Culberts Bay
YAMACRAW BEACH
Port New Providence

Winton Heights
Fox Hill
Winton Meadows
Yamacraw Road
Eastern Estates
Yamacraw Hill Estates

Long Cay
North Cay
Silver Cay
SAUNDER'S BEACH
Brown's Point
Goodman's Point

Long Point

PARADISE BEACH
Straw Market
Start
NASSAU
Fort Charlotte
Govern House
Seafood
Aquarium
The Grove
Acaviak Cay
COLONIAL BEACH
Delaporte Point

Queen's College
Village S.C.
Regatta Park
St. Augustine's Monastery
Sandiland Village
Charles S.C.
Glenston
Gardens Nassau East
Prince
Highbury Park
Kensington Gardens
Pinewood Estates
Malcolm Creek

Hospital
Centreville
Englerston
Fort Fincastle
Boyd
Rossell

Government Building
Chippingham
Stapleton Gardens
Oakes Field Golf Course
Oakes Field
Sunshine
Golden Gates
Mall on the Marathon
Golden Gates S.C.
South Beach Estate East
South Beach Estate West
SOUTH BEACH
South Beach Rd

Cable Beach
CABLE BEACH
Cartuby's Café
Hobby Horse Race Track
Lake Cunningham
John F. Kennedy Drive
36
Lake Killarney

NEW PROVIDENCE

Harold Ground
Wilson Pond
35
Miller Heights
Gladstone Road
Coral Park Ranch

Bonefish Pond

Cay Point

Rock Point
The Caves
28

Gambier Village
Road
Tropical Gardens
Windsor Field

Nassau International Airport

Carmichael Village
Coral Heights

Coral Harbour Road
Shopping Centre

Bacardi Rum Distillery
Bacardi Rum Plant

Millars Boat Harbour
Guana Cay
Millars Sound

Fishing Cays

Northwest Point
LOVE BEACH
Coral Gardens
Old Fort Point
Old Fort Bay
Old Fort
20
Mt. Pleasant
Mt. Pleasant

Ocean Hole
Adelaide Rd
Coral Harbour
Corry Sound
Fleming Point

Coral Harbour Golf Course
Royal Bahamas Defence Base

Road Adelaide
Adelaide Village
ADELAIDE BEACH

South West Bay

Creek Point
Mt. Pleasant Marina
Lyford Cay
Lyford Cay Golf Course
Simms Point
Clifton Point
Clifton Bluff
Clifton House (Ruins)
West Bay Street
South West
29
Clifton Pier
Old Fort (Ruins)
Clifton Bay

Welcome!

This guidebook combines the interests and enthusiasms of two of the world's best-known information providers: Insight Guides, who have set the standard for visual travel guides since 1970, and Discovery Channel, the world's premier source of non-fiction television programming. It aims to help you see the best of the Bahamas – a scattering of 2,700 coral-based pearls of land between the Atlantic and the Caribbean with enough romantic islands to last any traveller a lifetime. Only 30 of the islands are inhabited, and even the busiest are still peaceful by Continental standards.

'Having been raised in a quiet farming and fishing community in Canada, I found adjustment to Bahamian island life practically effortless,' says **Deby Nash**, Insight's correspondent in the Bahamas. Deby lived in Nassau from 1986, working as a teacher and journalist, before moving to Freeport, Grand Bahama, in the summer of 2000. Nassau, she says, is remarkably international. 'The streets are filled with people from every corner of the world, the shops are stocked with international fragrances and fashions, and Bahamians, in both Nassau and Freeport, are as stylish as residents of cities 10 times the size.'

Deby has aimed to illustrate some of the diversity of Nassau in her city itinerary in this book. But she has also designed other itineraries that will reveal the seductive, slow pace of island life, concentrating on the key destinations of New Providence, Paradise Island, Grand Bahama and its city of Freeport, Eleuthera, Harbour Island and Spanish Wells.

Wherever you go, you will be welcome, and if you follow the itineraries in this book you will enjoy the highlights of the Bahamas, together with the simple hospitality and open-door warmth of the islands' residents.

C O N T E N T S

Pages 2/3:
The island
of Exuma

Pages 8/9:
Lady Masons of
Holmes Rock,
Grand Bahama

Shopping, Dining & Nightlife

Calendar of Events

Practical Information

Maps

Lucayans and Legacies

A confused Christopher Columbus stumbled on to San Salvador Island on October 12, 1492. It was obvious he had not found a short-cut to China as he had set out to do. The graceful, gentle, brown-skinned Amerindians who met him on shore bore no resemblance to the Orientals he had expected. The disappointed navigator would never know that this land of 'shallow seas', the Bahamas, was to become the gateway to a New World – one of riches beyond anyone's imaginings.

The Lucayan Amerindians had tended their islands in peace and tranquillity for more than 500 years before Columbus, but now that they had been discovered, they would soon be gone forever. The skilled fishermen – once perhaps 4,000 strong – had no resistance to the European diseases Columbus and company brought with them. A key decider in their downfall was the thin topsoil on these limestone and coral-based islands: because the land yielded neither gold nor bountiful harvests of fruits and vegetables, the Spanish

Lucayan Indians hunting giant turtles

decided that the islanders would have to compensate them with human labour. The brief notes most history books accord the Lucayans mention that they were 'recruited' by the Spanish to work in the nearby mines of Hispaniola (now Haiti and the Dominican Republic); many would die during the sea voyage. Depopulation through disease and slavery continued until little more than 25 years later, when the Lucayans were finally no more.

With the labour force depleted, and neither gold nor treasures to be had, the Bahamas would remain deserted for almost 100 years. Only Ponce de León, while looking for the fountain of youth, passed through the islands, including San Salvador. In 1513 he touched on what is today called Grand Bahama. He wrote in his journals of a fast-moving, warm current flowing past the islands: this turned out to be the Gulf Stream, which would eventually lead his ship to the coast of Florida.

Columbus arrives

A Growing Sanctuary

Settlement in this New World began in earnest only in the 17th century, and once again for all the wrong reasons. The British, like the Spanish, had recognised a potential in the region for creating fortunes for themselves – not from land, but from the misfortunes of others. The slave trade was now in Africans. And poor or no experience in navigation, paired with treacherous shoals and well-armed galleons, made piracy a low-maintenance, high-return business. Rival slavers stole readily from each other.

The early 1600s was also a time of religious turmoil. The Anglican Church had been founded by Henry VIII, and British Puritan Congregationists, who acknowledged no higher power than the Bible or God, were looking for somewhere to practise their religion without fear.

William Sayle, a Puritan former governor of Bermuda, was among those who set sail seeking religious freedom. With few navigational skills, some 70 of his crew were shipwrecked off the north coast of Eleuthera. To this day, you will find a cave in North Eleuthera where these Eleutheran Adventurers are said to have gathered for shelter and prayers.

But the land had not improved, and the Puritans found it hard to survive. Many of them, including Sayle, were forced to leave. He returned to Bermuda in 1657, but came back frequently to the

The Woodes Rogers family

Bahamas, still looking for a permanent settlement. One island he discovered had excellent potential, particularly with its natural harbour. This was New Providence, on which the city of Nassau is now located, and thanks to development by Sayle it was to become the magnet of the Caribbean for the next 350 years.

Early Nassau

More and more Bermudian Puritans began moving to New Providence from Eleuthera as word spread that the farming and fishing were easier there. The island community continued to grow, though it was plagued by lawlessness. It soon became a base for piracy, the slave trade, and cannibalising ship-wrecked galleons. Even the notorious pirate Blackbeard is said to have been a frequent Nassau visitor.

A female pirate

In the territorial tug-of-war between England and Spain, New Providence was attacked as many as four times in 25 years, and Nassau was burned to the ground by the Spaniards.

Eventually the British got the upper hand and in 1718 Captain Woodes Rogers, Royal Governor, arrived to take control of the colony, which was now under the direct authority of the Crown. During his tenure, he accurately predicted that he would be remembered because 'he expelled the pirates and restored commerce.'

Prejudice and Politics

Woodes Rogers also put in place the first steps towards a representative Bahamian Assembly. Bahamians, like their neighbours to the north, the North American colonists, had had no representation in government. Their lives until then had been directly controlled by British agents of the Crown. The first representative Assembly was convened in 1729, and thereafter rarely missed a session, making it one of the longest continually meeting assemblies in the New World.

The issue of colour was becoming increasingly important on the islands. The representative Assembly appeared to represent only the narrow interests of powerful Nassuvians, who were mostly of European extraction and therefore white. But the black population was increasing fast, and Bahamians of African descent were finding that no matter what country they came from, they had one major factor uniting them: oppression by the white minority.

Britain outlawed slavery at home in 1772, but the new liberty took time to spread to the Bahamas. As the fires of revolution mounted in the 13 American colonies, men with religious and ideological convictions made their way to the Bahamas once again. Among them was Frank Spence, an enslaved man who arrived in 1780 with a group of British Loyalists. He saved up enough money to buy his freedom a year later, and eventually began the first Baptist congregation in the Bahamas.

Loyalists and Emancipation

At the end of the American War of Independence in 1783, the terms of the Treaty of Versailles included the British exchange of Florida for the Bahamas. The losing Loyalists fled north and south; those who came to the Bahamas brought with them thousands of slaves, and were briefly successful at establishing cotton plantations. However, this love affair with the land was once again to be short-lived as problems quickly developed with insect infestation, overplanting, and deforestation.

In 1807 the slave trade was prohibited throughout all British possessions and on British ships, and the British navy began to free enslaved people on those vessels they captured, adding considerable numbers to the former plantation slaves living on the islands. This growing population now had a country, and even property, but few skills and few options to relocate. After all, America was still adjusting to its new status, and its uneasy truce between the races held few prospects for immigrants.

As a result some freed men made their homes in New Providence, but many preferred the isolation and relative lack of interference in the Out Islands, briefly called the Family Islands. These people integrated relatively well with the original white settlers, largely because the latter had been cut off from European influence. In isolation, often with enslaved people as their only company, these first white Bahamian settlers had developed a relationship based on mutual survival and respect. The legacy, centuries later, is the unique character of the Bahamian people.

But the American Civil War (1861–1865) saw the return of smuggling to the Bahamas. With the growing number of lighthouses, shipwrecks were fewer and thus becoming less profitable. Bahamians were asked to show their support

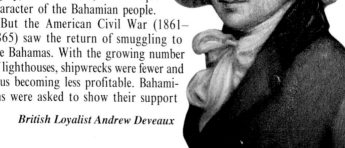

British Loyalist Andrew Deveaux

Unloading cotton in 1865

for Abraham Lincoln by blockading the southern ports to stop black-market activity. But easy money was to be had from smuggling, and stopping it wasn't easy. Fast boats smuggled goods to Florida – to consumers who, ironically, had only recently been the slave-masters of their new suppliers.

With peace and the signing of the Apomattox Treaty in 1865 the fragile Bahamas economy once again took a sharp downturn. The humble but legitimate sponging industry briefly became the country's largest money-earner, but bigger dollars were to be had elsewhere. Many skilled Bahamians contracted themselves out to citrus farms and plantations in the United States, especially in the Florida area. The exodus was to continue until the tourism boom of the 1950s began to take effect. Many contract workers never returned, creating a family bond between Florida and the Bahamas that continues even today.

Prohibition and the Windsors

For those Bahamians who remained at home, the US Prohibition laws of 1920 created instant prosperity. Bootlegging on the high seas made for good business. And bars with free-flowing liquor attracted the adventurous, creating the Bahamas' jazz age of the 1930s.

Prohibition was repealed in 1933. Once more, it looked like the 'in' place would soon be on its way out of favour. But in 1940, the arrival of the Duke and Duchess of Windsor, following the former's abdication from the British throne, focused world attention back on the Bahamas. The man who had given up his crown for the woman he loved lent an air of sophistication and – albeit tinged – respectability to the tiny colony.

In World War II, black and white Bahamians alike volunteered to serve in the Canadian and British West Indies forces. The British and American high command chose a deserted section of the western part of New Providence to construct an enormous pilot training centre for the war effort. Black construction workers became incensed when they found they were being paid less than white men working on the same project. In one of few public displays of violence in the country's history, they rioted on Bay Street, the bastion of the establishment. Several were killed in clashes, and offices and bar rooms were looted or burned to the ground. The workers eventually secured their raise, and the airbase was eventually built. After the war it became Nassau International Airport.

The Windsors in Nassau

At about the same time – 1942 – Canadian-born gold magnate and philanthropist Sir Harry Oakes was brutally murdered. With the Duke of Windsor overseeing the investigation, charges were soon brought against Oakes's son-in-law. After a sensational trial, the accused was acquitted. Today, the case of the murder of one of the richest men in the British Empire still remains unsolved.

From Colony to Commonwealth

And then the war was over. It seemed everyone was seeking ways to escape the harsh realities of a post-war adjustment. Many Bahamians were still working as farm labourers in the US, but the opportunities were becoming scarce.

Meanwhile, an invasion of another sort was taking place back home. British investors began buying up huge chunks of Bahamas real estate as fears of increased taxation grew with the election of the British Labour Party. And, closer at hand, Americans, who now had both the desire and the means to travel, were discovering the Bahamas could be a fast and inexpensive weekend getaway.

Sensing a trend, astute businessman Sir Stafford Sands created a National Development Board in 1950, which would market the Bahamas as a year-round vacation spot. Nassau's harbour was dredged to provide docking to even the largest ships in the expanding Caribbean cruise-ship market.

Sands also helped put in place bank secrecy laws comparable to those of Switzerland, with attractive tax concessions that would establish the Bahamas as an international banking centre. For the first time in centuries, two industries – tourism and offshore banking – ensured a legitimate and promising future for Bahamians. They continue even today to provide the Bahamas with the second highest per capita income (the Cayman Islands has the highest) in the Caribbean region.

The new-found affluence of the early 1960s coincided with the rise of party politics. Women won the right to vote in 1962, and they were a significant force in the creation of the Progressive Liberal Party (PLP) by Bahamians of African descent. The PLP became an alternative to the United Bahamian Party (UBP), which consisted

Queen Elizabeth II with Gerald Cash and Sir Lynden Pindling

largely of wealthy white Bahamian businessmen, who were known as the 'Bay Street Boys'.

Lynden Pindling's PLP won the 1967 election with the largest number of voters ever enfranchised: a black majority government had been won without bloodshed or outside interference. So began the 'Quiet Revolution' – the non-violent philosophy of the PLP to bring in majority rule. Two years later the Constitution was revised, and Pindling became the first Prime Minister. By the early 1970s, the UBP had aligned itself with splinter groups and become the Free National Movement. They assisted the PLP in negotiating the terms of the first independent constitution. On 10 July 1973, after 325 years as a colony of Britain, the Bahamas achieved independence.

Prime Minister Pindling was knighted by the Queen in 1983, but his government's travel and tourism explosion had brought with it some negative side-effects, notably in the trade of cocaine, for which the Bahamas are ideally positioned. Close cooperation with American drug enforcement agencies has stemmed the tide.

Investment in tourist infrastructure has been huge. Nassau's Crystal Palace Resort and Casino cost $300 million before it opened in 1990. In the same year, the International Business Act became law, giving the Bahamas a special place in offshore banking.

On 19 August 1992, the opposition Free National Movement, with slogans like 'Deliverance' and 'Government in the Sunshine', became the Bahamas' second administration, breaking the 25-year-hold of the Progressive Liberal Party. Days later, Hurricane Andrew cut a devastating swath through the nation, hitting the island of Eleuthera hard.

In under 48 hours, new Prime Minister Hubert Ingraham's hurricane relief committee was already hard at work. It took just over one year to complete the restoration.

The Nassau Marriott Resort and Crystal Palace Casino

Historical Highlights

1492 Columbus arrives in the New World, at the island of Guanahani. He renames it San Salvador (Holy Saviour).

1513 Ponce de León discovers the Gulf Stream.

1647 Eleutheran Adventurers create the first republic of the New World.

1648 Cigatoo Island claimed by colonials and renamed Eleuthera, from the Greek word meaning Freedom.

1718 Britain sends Woodes Rogers as Royal Governor, to combat growing piracy and lawlessness in the new colony.

1729 The first representative Assembly is convened.

1772 Slavery is outlawed in Britain but not throughout the empire as a whole.

1776 First foreign invasion, by the United States, at Fort Montague.

1780 Frank Spence, a slave, arrives with a group of Loyalists. He creates a ministry that becomes the Bahamian Anglican Church.

1782 The second foreign invasion – the Spanish. They recapture the Bahamas as retribution for persistent piracy against their vessels.

1783 Immigration of American Loyalists after the Treaty of Versailles. Others flee to Nova Scotia, Canada, where the predominantly black Acadia University remains a popular choice among Bahamian students intent on studying abroad.

1793 Fort Fincastle built at New Providence's highest point.

1834 Slavery abolished throughout the British Empire, including the Bahamas.

1861–5 The Royal Victoria Hotel is built during the economic boom generated from smuggling goods to Florida during the American Civil War. After the war the economy takes a downturn.

1920–33 Rum-running and the Jazz Age flourish in the Bahamas during Prohibition until its repeal in 1933. This begins the prominence of the 'Bay Street Boys'.

1940s Fame and glamour return to the Bahamas as the Duke and Duchess of Windsor arrive.

1942 Canadian-born gold magnate and philanthropist Sir Harry Oakes is murdered.

1955 Wallace Groves, founder of the Grand Bahama Port Authority, designs and gets approval for the Hawksbill Creek Agreement, creating a tax-free haven which will become Freeport-Lucaya.

1960s Growth of black consciousness and creation of the Progressive Liberal Party (PLP).

1962 Women win the right to vote and are important in the creation of the Progressive Liberal Party (PLP).

1967 PLP wins elections and begins the 'Quiet Revolution' towards majority rule.

1973 On 10 July, the Bahamas achieves independence.

1977 The Bahamas' first radio and television system is introduced.

1982 Janet Bostwick becomes first female member of Parliament.

1992 On 19 August, the Free National Movement decisively beats the Pindling government, becoming the first new administration in 25 years.

1995 Atlantis Resort opens on Paradise Island.

1997 The Freeport Container Port opens in Grand Bahama, making it a major world trans-shipment centre.

1998 The Bahamas celebrates 25 years of independence; a second bridge linking Nassau to Paradise Island begins operation.

2001 The Nassau Straw Market burns down, for the third time since it began operating in 1901.

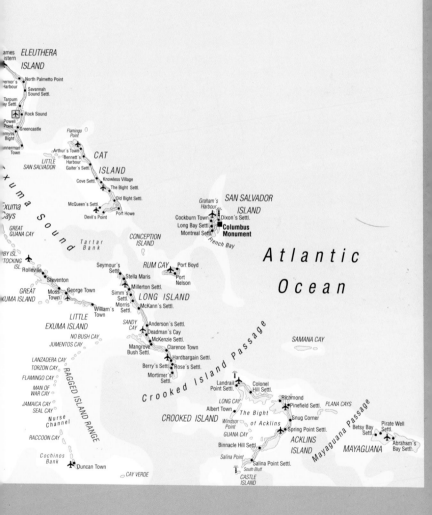

New Providence & Paradise

Only 200 miles (320km) from the Florida coastline, the island of New Providence is a half hour's flying time from Miami, 45 minutes from Fort Lauderdale, and one hour from Palm Beach. At 22 miles (35km) long and 7 miles (11km) wide, this former shipping colony has an infrastructure that was intended for horse and buggies only – as will quickly become apparent to any visitor. However, the traffic congestion is worthy of any big city, and many of the streets are without street signs. It's best to leave it to your cab or jitney driver to take you around the inner city of Nassau, as they know which streets are one-way (not all are marked).

Public transport is via jitney – a 32-seat Bahamian public bus. Otherwise, as an alternative to hiring your own taxi, you can always rent a motorcycle. By restricting your exploration to Bay Street, a main road which flows east and west along the shoreline, you can see most of the island without worrying about getting lost.

Most cruise ships dock at Nassau

The $1 fare on a jitney is the simplest. Be sure you have coins for the fare because the drivers will not give change. Jitneys can get you to most points of the island, but they cease operation after 6pm. Evening forays must be made by taxi (ask what the fare will be before setting off) or your hotel, which will arrange suitable transport to the more popular spots.

A hands-on-heart smile

1. Downtown Nassau

A horse and buggy ('surrey') ride and walking tour of Nassau's inner city, replete with international shops and boutiques, including the House of Parliament and the Straw Market.

The pulse of the city is Bay Street, Nassau's oldest and main thoroughfare. Taste a hearty traditional breakfast of fish broth and johnny cake at Conch Fritters Restaurant, opposite the venerable British Colonial Hilton, at No. 1 Bay Street, then walk off some of the calories by strolling the five short blocks along the main street, Bay Street, to Rawson Square.

Rawson Square, is the starting point for the horse and buggy (also called a surrey) tours. A bust of the first Bahamian Governor-General, Sir Milo Butler, is a popular photo opportunity here. Then hop on a **surrey** – some actually do have a fringe on top – and have the driver take you on a leisurely half-hour tour of the downtown area; fares start at around $10 per person.

This half-hour tour will provide you with a cultural

A surrey ride

and historical synopsis of the streets and buildings along the route, as well as identifying the flora and fauna indigenous to the Bahamas. Although the traffic might make you feel a bit apprehensive, neither the horses nor the Nassau car drivers seem to be at all nervous in each other's company, even in the rush hour. This tour is the perfect way to get an overview of the city centre when you first arrive.

The landmarks appear quickly in this small central area. The first of these is the **Garden of Remembrance**, which is located in Parliament Square, just off Parliament Street. With courthouses on one side, and the Nassau Public Library on the other, this tiny area is actually a cenotaph, commemorating the Bahamians who died in World Wars I and II.

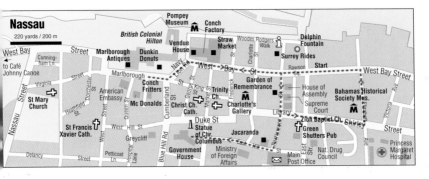

Nassau Public Library

After the surrey turns on to Shirley Street, which is second only to Bay Street in the amount of traffic, you'll see the **Nassau Public Library** on your left. Built in 1797, this octagonal-shaped building was formerly a jail. The library is still surrounded by small courtrooms, and you will probably see some clients sitting under the shade of a tree as they wait for their cases to be called. If you decide to browse around on your own, it would be well worth going inside the library. About a dozen of what used to be prison cells are now lined with books. If you ask, the librarian will also show you a rare collection of historical prints, colonial artefacts, and the Bahamian Collection – volumes written by and about Bahamians.

On the same side of Shirley Street, two blocks along and at the corner of Elizabeth Avenue, is the Bahamas **Historical Society Museum**. It has several displays depicting Bahamas history from pre-Columbian times – including Lucayan Amerindian artefacts – to the present. One block further down, on the right side of Shirley Street, is the **Princess Margaret Hospital**, the public hospital so named in honour of the Princess's visit in 1955.

The surrey will then make a left turn for a short trot down Bay Street, and take you back to where you began the tour. When you step out of the carriage, you will be looking at **Rawson** and **Parliament** squares, which contain the main Bahamian government offices. These include the House of Parliament, the Old Colonial Secretary Office, and the Supreme Court. You may want to sit in on a session in the latter (contact the Bahamas Tourist Office, tel: 302-2000, for details) and witness the old British system of justice in operation. A statue of Queen Victoria sits regally in the centre

Parliament Square

of Parliament Square. This is a popular area for performances by visiting musicians and musical groups.

Turn right (west) on to Bay Street and take a leisurely stroll past the duty-free fashion and jewellery shops. Just a few short blocks away, in the Market Plaza, is the Nassau **Straw Market**, a national landmark covering a full city block. First constructed in 1901, it was destroyed by fire in 1974 and replaced by another structure. That, too, fell victim to a fire in 2001, and has since been replaced by a temporary tent facility which is actually larger than its predecessors. Almost any handicraft you can imagine is to be found amongst the 500 stalls at this market, but most common are items made of straw or wood. Your best souvenirs will be straw-work collectibles made by vendors on the spot. Although haggling is frowned on in most storefront retail establishments, almost all the prices here are negotiable.

The **Pompey Museum** is practically next door. The present museum and art gallery was used during the 18th century for slave auctions. Today its artefacts and historical documents trace the process of slavery, abolition, and emancipation. The second storey contains paintings by Amos Ferguson, the Bahamas' most renowned and oldest living artist.

In the Straw Market

Follow the bend in the road, past the British Colonial Hilton, to the **Conch Fritters Restaurant**. With pale pastel decor and soothing jazz or *soca* coming through the unobtrusive sound system, it has a calming effect, especially if you have a light salad or seafood lunch while watching the noon-day crowds pass by.

After lunch, retrace your steps along Bay Street. You'll see several duty-free shops, with a wide selection of exclusive perfumes, watches and designer fashions. Turn right at Parliament Street and watch members of Parliament and barristers moving busily between the courts and the House of Parliament, which lie just behind the statue of Queen Victoria.

At the top of Parliament Street is the **Main Post Office**. There is no home mail delivery in the Bahamas; the thousands of metal postboxes you see are a valuable commodity, as residents can sometimes wait for more than a year for one to become available for rental. The Post Office mounts displays of arts, crafts, or historical events which are changed regularly. There are also special collectors' editions of stamps which make great souvenirs.

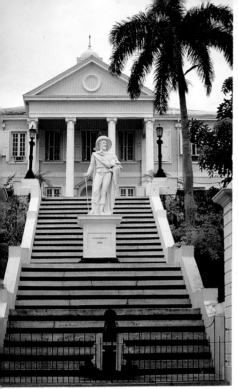

Government House

You can see the entrance to **Government House** from the Post Office steps. It is the Bahamas' version of Buckingham Palace, and the official residence of the Governor-General, the Queen's official representative in the islands. Two Defence Force officers, in white military dress, are at their ceremonial post at the entrance gates. Just past them, a white statue of Christopher Columbus stands on the steps of the House.

As you walk back down Parliament Street from the Post Office you might want to stop off and try some beer on tap at the 'very British' **Green Shutters Pub**. It's situated across the street from the **National Drug Council**, repository of one of the most innovative and comprehensive research collections available on Aids in the Caribbean region. The council's offices are open to the general public.

Near the bottom of the hill, not far from where you began your day in Nassau, is the **Parliament Café** (tel: 322-7387), housed in the Parliament Hotel. With its own Daiquiri bar, it offers comfortable indoor or outdoor seating. Its location also makes it a regular meeting place for parliamentarians and attorneys who like to hold their 'power lunches' here. An acoustic group serenades as you dine on anything from fresh pâté to guava duff. A traditional British tea for two – complete with delicate cucumber sandwiches and banana bread – is available in the afternoons.

If you would like a little more local flavour (and tempo) when it comes to your night-time entertainment, I recommend that you try an evening with Jay Mitchell and the Fine Tone Band, in the Palm Court Lounge of the British Colonial Hilton. Music ranges from jazz to James Brown to this recording artist's own calypsos. There's no admission charge for Mitchell's nightly foyer performance, but you will see a full house of very receptive fans, dancing or sipping on a rum-based 'Bahama Mama' or one of the other cocktails on offer from the bar.

Cocktails at Parliament Ca

2. To Paradise Island

A day that starts in Nassau and moves on to the 'Monaco of the Caribbean'. End the itinerary back on New Providence, in the Caribbean's largest casino, which is located on Cable Beach.

The character of Nassau has probably been moulded more by visitors to its shores than that of most countries. Nowhere is the impact of tourism more evident than in the heart of town. Just behind where the downtown surreys are stationed stands a signpost with arrows pointing in all directions. It graces the entrance to the **Tourist Information Centre**, which has every brochure and bulletin available about what there is to see and do on this and all the other Bahamian islands.

Paradise Island viewed from a plane

Beside it, and parallel to Bay Street – as well as stretching half its downtown length – is the **Woodes Rogers Walk**. You should begin your day here by watching for a while the magnificent cruise ships that regularly glide in and out along the waterfront. **Prince George Dock**, the largest port in the Caribbean, bustles with non-stop traffic as cruise ships from around the world jostle for berths every morning, their passengers pouring into the city in their thousands.

As you stroll along the walkway, you'll encounter vendors who arrived before sunrise to set up their stalls here or at the Straw

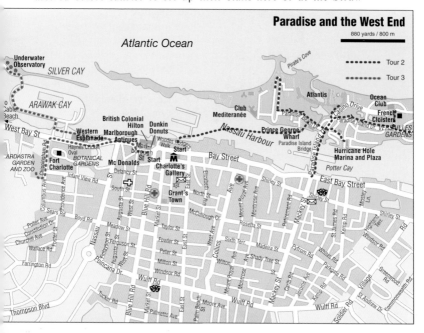

Crystal Palace Beach

Market further along. The market has rows and rows of colourful items made of straw, including hats, place mats, dolls, and baskets, along with elaborate wood carvings, and, of course, mounds of T-shirts. The vendors do a bustling business selling fresh fruits and the morning's catch, and will plait your hair into cornrows if you want to 'look Bahamian'.

Every half hour or so, a glass-bottomed boat loads up here, with passengers about to make a trip to visit the Sea Gardens — a protected marine park with a large variety of fish and corals. But you should be looking out for a different form of marine transport: at the same docking area is the **Paradise Island ferry**, which shuttles visitors to the island every 20 minutes, starting at 8am. The ferry route takes you to a number of points on Paradise Island, and then offers a return trip to the Straw Market or the cruise ship dock. This is the quick way to go, but do try the glass-bottomed boats and the smaller shuttles as well if you have the time; each has their own charm in the form of the boat pilots, and their reasonable rates are regulated.

Sometimes known as the 'Monaco of the Caribbean', **Paradise Island** had much humbler origins than its celestial title may suggest: the 826-acre (335-ha) retreat was called Hog Island by its early settlers, because at one time the island was mainly a home for pigs, with not very much else going on.

How things have changed. Apart from visitors arriving by ferry, cruising yachtsmen can dock at the 57-slip, full-service Hurricane Hole Marina. The island has championship golf and tennis courts spread throughout its 15 major hotels and condominium properties, and has more than 4,000 hotel rooms.

Although you may have to be a millionaire to live on Paradise Island, there are no such monetary restrictions for the visitor. It is truly a pedestrian's paradise and there are numerous quaint gift shops to browse in as you stroll around.

Shopping over, wander along any of the white sandy beaches, which are all within easy walking distance once you've arrived on the island. The clean, white sand goes on forever, and is becoming a popular place for movie-makers who want beautiful beach scenes with blue waves rippling into the sunsets. Try to end up at the west end of the island, on Paradise Beach, by which time you'll be ready for something to eat.

Conch, prepared Bahamian-style, is the island speciality, and Bahamians pride themselves on preparing their own variations of the recipe. Fritters, for example, can be made with either minced or chopped conch. I prefer the 'conchy' chopped conch, with coarsely chopped bits mixed into the spicy batter, though there are some who prefer the more subtle, ground-up version.

You can get some good conchy conch fritters at the **Blue Marlin Restaurant**, located at the Hurricane Hole Shopping Plaza, which faces the marina of the same name. The Blue Marlin also remains the sole establishment on either New Providence or Paradise Island still offering what is known as a 'native show' most evenings, replete with glass-walking, limbo-dancing and fire-dancing.

On the opposite side of the shopping plaza, just a short distance across Harbour Drive, you'll find the multi-coloured **Bahama Craft Centre**. The wooden market houses around 100 booths packed with local art and craft work – an indoor version of the Bay Street Straw Market.

But don't linger here if you want to catch the magical **Cloisters Garden** before dusk. Leaving the craft centre and the shopping plaza, head back toward the Paradise Island Bridge, a few hundred yards/metres along turn east on to Paradise Island Drive (by the street sign). The walk along the dual carriageway takes about 15 minutes; it's a pleasant stroll past the Comfort Suites, an exclusive time-share resort at the corner of Paradise Island Drive.

The **Cloisters** are the remains of a 14th-century monastery imported to the United States from France by newspaper baron William Randolph Hearst in the 1920s. Forty years later, grocery-chain heir Huntington Hartford bought them and had them installed at the top of a hill overlooking Nassau Harbour. They have become a popular venue for weddings; couples may organise a ceremony through the Ministry of Tourism's People-to-People programme, with a Bahamian minister officiating. Tasteful arrangements can be made for a simple and romantic outdoor ceremony.

The Cloisters: an import from 14th-century France

Cold embrace in the Versailles Garden

The **Versailles Garden**, also the creation of Hartford, is located between the Cloisters and the posh Ocean Club. It is a formal garden, terraced into seven levels, with a number of marble and bronze statues.

You will have seen the towering 34-acre (14-ha) **Atlantis** resort in the distance, even before crossing the bridge to Paradise Island. Don't leave the island without taking a tour of the world's largest salt-water aquarium, which includes an underground version of the mythical lost island of Atlantis. The property also has a large casino and 38 restaurants and lounges, as well as several luxury gift shops.

Watching the sunset while walking back over the 70-ft (20-metre) high, 1,700-ft (520-metre) long **Paradise Island Bridge** is a magical experience. A second bridge was built to link Paradise Island to the mainland in 1998. Should you prefer some local colour, hop on board a jitney at the Nassau end of the bridge. Bus stops on New Providence are sometimes marked – as at this end of the bridge – but often just an upraised arm will get the driver's attention. And don't worry about causing confusion any time your arm is raised; these drivers can distinguish a customer from someone waving to a friend. Located in front of the small shopping plaza, the jitney will take you back downtown. The fare is $1; make sure you have the exact change. The bus will stop near the British Colonial Hilton, at the western end of Nassau's shopping mile. Here you should get off the first bus, and on to one marked Cable Beach – you'll have to pay again. The beach is a direct route along Bay Street, with a scenic drive along the coastline which takes about 15 minutes (or 10 minutes by cab).

You should ask to stop at **The Nassau Marriott Resort and Crystal Palace Casino**. At 35,000 sq. ft (3,250 sq. metres), this is the largest casino in the Caribbean. It has 750 slot machines, 60 blackjack tables, 11 craps tables, American and European roulette, baccarat, and other interesting ways to 'lose your shirt' on a table – including horseracing. In the casino, you can experiment with everything from a 5-cent, one-armed bandit to the far more pricey baccarat tables. And if you don't know what you are doing but would like to learn, the casinos on Paradise Island and Cable Beach provide free gaming lessons, with complimentary cocktails.

A matter of luck

3. Western Attractions

Excursions through the most popular attractions on New Providence, to the west of downtown Nassau. See map on page 25.

Start your morning early with a decadent buffet breakfast at the **Portofino Café**, located in the ground-floor lobby of the British Colonial Hilton in downtown Nassau, at No. 1 Bay Street. There is plenty of choice, from traditional eggs, toast or bagels, to grits and fish concoctions, along with local fruit and juices – even moist banana bread. If you prefer to have just a quick bite, it's just a few steps to Nassau's sole **Dunkin Donuts** outlet. Located across the street from the hotel, this is one of the oldest counter restaurants in Nassau, and is often used by local people as a reference point for giving directions. The Cable Beach jitneys, whose route follows the shoreline towards the western part of the island, regularly stop at this spot, making the corner cafeteria the commuter's best friend. Breakfast muffins and coffee do a good business here, and service is no-frills but prompt.

You may have begun to feel a bit daunted by the apparent paucity of affordable restaurants in the city's urban centre. At this end of Bay Street, however, finding somewhere cheap to eat is not really a problem. Just three buildings away – two past Conch Fritters Restaurant – you'll find McDonald's; two other fast-food outlets, KFC and Burger King, are just around the bend of Bay Street, at the most western end of the Bay Street shopping mile. All of these eating establishments serve breakfast, and have even Bahamianised a few items

Fresh conch for sale

to provide a bit of variation to the standard monotonous menu.

The Cable Beach jitneys will be visible when you walk out of any of these restaurants. Hop on board, and ask the driver to let you off at the **Fish Fry** at **Arawak Cay**, located about five minutes' drive away. On the opposite side of West Bay Street from where you disembark you will see a fruit and vegetable stand, at the corner of the side street called Chippingham Road. The stall vendors can help you identify some of the local fruits in season. You may see your first sugar-apple, sapodilla, guava, mango – or even tamarind and soursop. Guineps are plentiful, too; they look like a bunch of grapes with a tough green covering, but a bite through the hard outer shell releases a sweet juice. Be adventurous – here's your chance to try things you won't find at home.

Behind the fruit stall is **Fort Charlotte**, one of 12 fortifications in the Nassau area. It was built in 1789 by a representative of the British crown, Lord Dunmore, who was very unpopular at the time – especially with the loyalists who had just arrived from the north after their embarrassing defeat in the American revolutionary war. He named the fort in honour of Queen Charlotte, wife of King George III. Fort Charlotte is still in excellent condition and has never seen a shot fired in battle. Local guides are available to show you the water-less moat, drawbridge, ramparts, and dungeons.

Just southwest of the fort are the **Botanical Gardens**, featuring more than 600 species of flowering trees and shrubs. There is a recreated Lucayan village in the grounds, and an impressive look-out point from where visitors can see everything for miles around – from the garden and village areas, to the hills and valleys of Centreville Nassau.

The **Ardastra Gardens and Zoo** is next door. It comprises 5 acres (2 ha) of beautiful, tropical gardens, complete with iguanas, monkeys, snakes, lizards, and birds, including the rare Bahamas parrot, and the world-famous marching flamingos. These 'ballerinas in pink' really do respond to the command of a 'drill sergeant' caretaker. You can have a photo taken standing among them, should you attend the shows, which take place three times a day. The more interesting trees are labelled with informative plaques. You'll also see Bahamian fruits growing in their natural habitat, and plants like mahogany, frangipani and cabbage palm.

Back at Arawak Cay, create your own lunch from the selection of the fresh fruits and conch dishes, prepared while you wait. A giveaway that you are a tourist is the way you pronounce the name of this latter national staple – be sure to call it 'conk' like the locals do. The most popular raw versions of conch are in salad –

Birds of a feather made with chopped conch, onions, tomatoes, green pepper, and lime juice – and 'scorched conch' – where the conch meat is not burned, but tenderised with a meat hammer, and then plopped in plastic bags, along with lemon juice and hot pepper sauce.

This is a great place for later, too, when city workers stop by for a cool beer and a snack on the way home. There are no knives or forks for your conch snack – you just put your hand in the bag and tear off a piece of the meat. Conch is high-protein and low-calorie – a dieter's delight. The calories obviously increase a bit if you eat whole conchs fried in batter ('cracked' conch), but the crispy batter and chewy consistency of the dish make it worth sampling.

Most stalls have eclectic decor and seating for their customers, so you can

Preparing the catch of the day

usually eat at the place where you choose your seafood. Fishermen also have the day's catch available – it will probably be grouper, snapper or crayfish (lobster). If you are near your hotel, it is not uncommon to buy something fresh like this and ask the chef at your hotel to prepare it for you.

Along with the food stalls there is the Heritage Village component of the cay. The site has grown to be the location of choice for national cultural festivals throughout the year. The village has a story-teller's porch, a bandstand, and a well manicured village green to accommodate the festival goers.

If you would rather walk back to the downtown area from Arawak Cay, you should allow an hour or so. If it's a Friday or Saturday, you'll probably see a cricket match in progress at the famous **Haynes Cricket Oval**, on the sloping green just below the fort.

On the opposite side of Bay Street, facing the water, is a raised open space called the **Western Esplanade**. It actually runs into the fish and vegetable markets at its far end, at the junction of West Bay Street and Chippingham Road. Although it just looks like a patch of green during the week, on most Saturday and Sunday afternoons locals pitch tents, fire up the charcoal, and have 'cookouts' here. Fish, chicken, conch, and spare ribs are prepared the way Bahamians like them – a bit spicier than the watered-down restaurant fare – and full meals are sold in styrofoam containers for a few dollars a plate. If you've managed a weekend visit to Nassau, try to get to one of these events. It's a great way to see local people relaxing when they're not dressed to impress for Bay

Nassau straw work

Local arts and crafts

Street. Besides, you know the food is always good when the chef is eating it too.

The next stop is **Marlborough Antiques**. It has one of the world's best collections of early photos of the Bahamas. Antiques, too, of course, as well as an interesting selection of books, jewellery, writing paper, and works of local Bahamian artists. A co-owner, Brent Malone, is a distinguished artist in his own right, whose oil-on-canvas 'junkanoo' scenes portraying Caribbean parades, grace many an international collection.

Now that you are back in downtown, you can visit more than a dozen art galleries and museums dotting Bay Street and its side-streets. The celebrations marking Columbus' arrival in the New World in 1492 sparked something of a cultural rebirth in the region, giving impetus to the Bahamian artistic community. Fortunately for the visitor, this means that many original works of art are available and affordable. Some of the more interesting ones are to be found among the bric-à-brac of the Straw Market, which was visited as part of Itinerary 1 *(see page 23)*, but be sure you give yourself a good few hours to browse there.

For the kind of souvenirs that you immediately know will be just right, try **Charlotte's Gallery**, on Charlotte Street (just off Bay, and opposite the Straw Market). It promotes lesser-known as well as established Bahamian artists, whose junkanoo paintings, done in brilliant acrylics, may be the best kind of souvenir. On display are mini-lithographs, greetings cards, pottery, and even miniature pieces of stained-glass art.

On Parliament Street is the **Kennedy Gallery**, which exhibits and sells the work of local and international artists. And a stone's throw from the two Paradise Island bridges, in the shopping centre on East Bay Street is the **Nassau Art Gallery**, with watercolour prints and hand-painted porcelain plates that will be snapped up by collectors. Both of these properties are fine examples of good, small, local galleries, which are happy to sell both art works and souvenirs.

If you miss the month-long **Junkanoo in June** festivities at Nassau's Arawak Cay, or the major Boxing Day and New Year's Day parades *(see pages 76–77)*, then **Doongalik Studios** may be the next best thing. Located on Village Road, about a mile (2 km) from the downtown area, the studio sell arts and crafts exclusively dedicated to the Junkanoo themes of colour, drums and dance.

Calypso till you can't

You will probably want to return to your hotel for a well-earned rest and a shower to revive you after a busy day's exploring, then it will be time for the evening's entertainment. Why not head back out to Cable Beach. Hop on the bus just around the corner from the Junkanoo Expo on Prince George Wharf, at the stretch of the road separating Arby's and the British Colonial Hilton, and you will have a leisurely ride westwards along Bay Street, towards the Cable Beach strip, otherwise known as the Bahamian Riviera. Cable Beach, incidentally, got its name from the trans-oceanic cable that extended from Nassau to just north of Palm Beach, Florida. Today, the cable continues to provide the telephone link between the United States and the Bahamas.

Hop off the bus halfway along West Bay Street, near Saunders Beach, to dance the night away at the **Zoo** – the largest nightclub in the Bahamas. The entrance fee isn't cheap and it doesn't open until after 9pm, but there's a restaurant with reasonably priced snacks and meals, where you can bide your time until the dancing starts.

If you started your evening excursion a little earlier and you're not all shopped out, you could try the massive indoor promenade that connects the **Nassau Marriott Resort** with hotels at each end. There are exclusive dress and jewellery stores, duty-free liquor shops, and just about everything from tobacco stores to hairdresser's salons. The prices reflect the locale, however, and are rather high. Either window-shop or come prepared to buy a Paris or Rome original.

Among the shops here is Androsia, which sells brilliantly-hued batik clothing and souvenirs produced on the island of Andros. This is one of the few gift shops (Island Tings, in downtown Bay Street is another) selling Bahamian products exclusively, with works from other Bahamian islands, as well as Andros.

Have your sunset dinner on the terrace of **Café Johnny Canoe**, next to the Nassau Beach Hotel. The staff are friendly, and the decor is rustic, with jewel-coloured junkanoo art interspersed among black-and-white photos of the Bahamas of yesteryear. This place serves the best broiled grouper on the island. A three-piece combo plays Bahamian rake 'n' scrape, and a junkanoo group, replete with colourful costumes, 'rushes' through the restaurant, to the rhythm of the heated goatskin drums and cowbells.

Try the best broiled grouper

4. Around the Island

A long day's driving tour around the coastline of New Providence, taking in some smaller settlements and beachside bistros. When night falls, the dancing is non-stop at Nassau's most popular local disco.

There are a dozen major hotels in the downtown area of Nassau. Each has mini-scooters available for rent. The scooter guides will provide you with a map, helmet, and a full tank of gas. That will be all you need – excluding your suntan lotion and camera, of course – as you follow this itinerary to tour the island of New Providence at your leisure.

Before heading for the outskirts, there are some historical sites you won't want to miss. Park your scooter near the **Main Post Office** in East Street, and visit some of them. A few minutes from this part of the city centre there is an interesting collection of historical landmarks. Located off Shirley Street, on Elizabeth Avenue, are the 65 steps of the **Queen's Staircase**, each representing a year of Victoria's reign (1837–1901). Carved out of solid limestone by slaves in the 18th century, it was originally built to provide access from the town to the fort.

At the top is **Fort Fincastle**, shaped like a paddlewheel steamer.

The Queen's Staircase

Built in 1793 by Lord Dunmore, this fort offers a spectacular view from its lighthouse. Beside it is the **Water Tower.** Built in 1928, the tower still maintains the city's water pressure and, at 216 ft (65 metres) above sea level, it is the island's highest point. A lift takes you to the observation deck for a panoramic view of New Providence.

Now you're ready to return to your scooter and move out of the city. Go west along Bay Street, past Dunkin Donuts and Marlborough Antiques. As you drive away from the downtown area, the shoreline will always be on your right. Passing stately mansions built in the 19th century, you will notice the chain of hotel properties lining Cable Beach, the Nassau Marriott Resort being the largest.

Continuing west, you will see a **golf course** on your left.

Nassau Marriott Resort

Built in 1929 by Robert Trent, Jr, it is a popular par 72, 18-hole course. On the right side of the dual carriageway, at the roundabout, is **Goodman's Bay**, the unofficial entrance to the Cable Beach area, and itself a public beach. Power walkers and joggers are common here, and the spot is very popular with the aerobics set.

This section of the island is ideal for walkers. Small footpaths have been etched into the promenade that separates West Bay Street's east and west traffic flow. Ample shade is provided by arching casuarina trees, and pedestrians can walk for miles without worrying about the hazards of traffic.

Continue on, past the Cable Beach casino strip, stopping at **Capriccio's Cafe** for some homemade ice cream. Located at the Swanks' roundabout, this tiny café-cum-delicatessen also makes several different kinds of pasta. The success of this long established little place, situated among a chain of major hotel complexes and private villas, is down to its simple ambiance, good service and authentic Italian flavour.

After another 2 miles (3 km) you arrive at **Delaporte Point**, which has its own beach. Here you could take the opportunity to hire a different form of transport: hop off your scooter and on to a jet-ski to fly along miles of uncluttered beach while getting a close-up view of the numerous sailboats and windsurfers. For the more adventurous, parasailing is also available here: a nylon, parachute-like sail is hooked to a boat that pulls you aloft and zooms around while you get a bird's-eye view of the island.

Wave runners

The **Caves** are a further 2 miles (3 km) along Bay Street. Developed naturally out of soft limestone, they have the arrival of Prince Alfred of England in 1861 inscribed on their walls. Not far away, on the left side, is Blake Road, which leads into John F. Kennedy Drive and the **Nassau International Airport**. When the current $60-million expansion project is completed, this airport will have the largest and best-equipped customs and immigration pre-clearance facilities in the region.

But stay on Bay Street, because **Gambier Village** is just around the bend. The village was originally settled by liberated Africans after the abolition of slavery in 1807, and descendants of the island's oldest settlers still live here.

Traveller's Rest will probably tempt you to stop for a bit. Only about 10 minutes' drive from Cable Beach, the relaxed, island-flavoured restaurant and bar is a favourite watering-hole. It is said

Seagrape Boutique

that every once in a while, all Nassuvians make their way here. Androsian print table-cloths, local artwork, and murals festoon the walls. You'll probably see some patrons playing backgammon or Connect Four at one of the tables on the terrace. Adjoining the Traveller's Rest is the attractive **Seagrape Boutique**, which sells everything from Androsia fashions to handpainted jewellery and T-shirts. Browse around, and get that extra tube of sunscreen that you probably need by now.

Minutes away are the **Compass Point Studios**, used by the likes of Mick Jagger, Julio Iglesias and other recording artists. On either side of the winding road are the private estates of some of the more well-to-do inhabitants of the island. Between here and the next residential area, extending for about a ¼ mile (½ km) along the shore, is **Love Beach**, a picnic spot popular with local people.

Contrast this with the next residential area, **Lyford Cay**, where your neighbours – if you've got a few million dollars – could be Sean Connery and Arthur Hailey. Princess Diana used to be among the occasional guests who came to indulge in this exclusive enclave's luxury, country-club atmosphere. Nelson Mandela has also stayed here. At the entrance is a gate guarded 24 hours a day, so unless you have a special invitation, don't even try to get in. You can, however, browse around the small shopping centre located just outside the security gates.

Now leave the shopping centre, go round the roundabout and up the hill. You'll be passing a few residential areas, including **Mount Pleasant**, which was once the living quarters for the Lyford Cay service staff, but is now a middle-class suburb for Bahamians of all professions. **Clifton Point** occupies a sharp curve that veers to the left, indicating that you have reached the westernmost tip of the island. As you continue past here, you'll notice the Clifton Pier Power Station on the left-hand side. This facility provides electricity for the entire western end of New Providence Island.

It is at this point that Bay Street finally changes to Southwest Road.

As you continue your drive, you'll see the Clarion Resort South Ocean, one of the newer resorts on the island. Stop off and get yourself a cool Yuma

A chance to push the boat out

West Bay St Beach

Yuma to quench your thirst. This is a delicious concoction made with pineapple juice, a tablespoon of Drambuie and a tablespoon of Yuma Gold, the sugar-cane liqueur made on Long Island, Bahamas. To this is added a teaspoon each of blue Curaçao and Grenadine. Lovely, but lethal in large quantities.

As you resume the tour, the road will continue on to become Adelaide Road. Although the road changes its name you shouldn't worry about getting lost: you're always on the same major route. Don't be tempted to meander down any of the unmarked side-streets, though – most lead to residential areas.

A signpost announces the historical **Adelaide Village** turn-off on your right, but keep on going; the ruins of historic slave huts are located in this area, but are hard to find, even for the locals. If you would like more information about the ruins, call the **Bahamas National Trust** (tel: 393-1317). This is a non-profit organisation responsible for the preservation of Bahamian places of historic interest and natural beauty.

Continue along the Adelaide Road until it becomes Carmichael Road after you go across the roundabout at **Coral Harbour**. This is where the Bahamas Defence Force – the Bahamian version of the Canadian Mounties and the US Marines, all in one – have their main base.

Go through this intersection, continuing straight on along Carmichael Road. A few miles along there will be a sign on the right, announcing the entrance to the **Bacardi Rum Distillery**. This is worth the detour; turn right, and take a half hour or so to visit the property. There's a small building just inside the Bacardi grounds, with a bar where visitors can sample some of the different blends of the world-famous rum.

After this brief stop, go back to the Carmichael Road intersection and turn right. Keep on Carmichael Road until you reach the

Bahamian building

traffic light at the junction of Carmichael and **Blue Hill Road**. This is a fairly densely populated suburban area, with not much of historical note; but you do get a good impression of middle-class Bahamian lifestyle here.

Turn left at the T-junction on to Blue Hill Road, and then take the second right, which will put you on Soldier Road. The next set of traffic lights will indicate the intersection of Soldier and Robinson roads. Turn right at the traffic lights; the road now becomes Prince Charles Avenue.

Continue all the way along to the absolute end of the road. You are now at the eastern end of the island, called **McPherson's Bend**. Enjoy the fresh tang of the sea as you continue along the shoreline for about 6 miles (9 km). This drive along the shore is visually spectacular, as are the opulent homes of the upper-middle-class people who live here.

By the time you reach Old Fort Beach, named simply **Montagu** by local people, you have come three-quarters of the way around the island. This is the last open area before Paradise Island, and second only to the Western Esplanade (on West Bay Street) as the most popular local beach for 'cook-outs' – the outdoor, weekend, public barbecues – with chicken, seafood dishes and all kinds of pastries on sale.

Here also is **Fort Montagu**, the oldest of the three forts on New Providence, which was built in 1741 from local limestone. You might want to try a dish of conch salad at the **Poop Deck**, the terrace bar overlooking Nassau Harbour. On the opposite side of Bay Street from the Poop Deck is the **Pink Pearl Café**. This is a restored, two-storey, colonial building which dates back to the 1880s, and now has live jazz in the evening as a background to the excellent fusion Caribbean cuisine.

Alternatively, you could try a serenade at the **Vintage Club**, in the Buena Vista Restaurant on Delancy Street, in the city centre. Live jazz, both traditional and contemporary, is on offer at the club, along with a sumptuous dinner.

However, at this point you might want to return to your hotel to relax for a while before you decide on the evening's activities. This time you should let someone else do the driving, and

Conch Salad

take a taxi to the **Family Island Lounge**, a local nightclub a bit off the main thoroughfare, on Soldier Road, that is very popular with Nassuvians. A live band is in attendance, the atmosphere is informal, and the dancing non-stop.

5. Mini Excursions

My own selection of the best half-day boat excursions to nearby islands and coral reefs. Remember to buy ingredients for a picnic lunch to bring with you.

Ready to get away from it all? Take the Getaway Cruise from the Calypso Dock, on Paradise Island, for a 35-minute scenic ride to **Blue Lagoon Island**. The triple-deck *M/V Calypso* drops you on this uninhabited island, which was the location for several scenes of the movie *Splash*. Free snorkelling gear is provided, and volleyball and table tennis are as strenuous a sport as you might want, as you laze the day away. The nature trails are short, and the fauna and flora extremely pretty.

If you've signed up for the educational 'Dolphin Encounter', you will be shown an introductory video about these creatures, followed by a brief question-and-answer period (did you know they have three stomachs?), during which live dolphins play around you as you stand in waist-deep water, or swim around your toes as you sit on a floating platform. Enjoy your prepared picnic lunch, then spend the afternoon swimming or snorkelling. The *M/V Calypso* also has a 3-hour dinner cruise, with a live band for dancing before and after the dinner of beef and fresh seafood.

Alternatively, get the **Beach Runners** to collect you from your hotel and carry you away on a scarab power-boat for a full- or half-day island-hopping exploration of what are described as 'remote sites on nearby islands'. Barbecued lunch and full bar are included in the price of the charter. The boats take up to 15 people.

For a glass-bottomed boat ride, check out the **Booze and Cruise Co. Ltd**, whose *Lucayan Queen* allows you to see underwater shipwrecks and a Bahama sea garden. The on-board entertainment includes a limbo-dancing contest, and the price of the trip covers unlimited cocktails and delicious snacks. The *Lucayan Queen* departs from the Paradise Island Dock at 1pm (the company organises a bus pick-up from Cable Beach) and returns at about 5pm (for details, tel: 393-3722).

You can also take a trip from New Providence to Spanish Wells, Harbour Island and Eleuthera via **Bahamas Fast Ferries**. The *Bo Hengy* is a 177-seat, air-conditioned catamaran

Dolphin encounters

A 'Booze and Cruise' boat

that makes the trip from the Paradise Island Bridge on New Providence to this island cluster in just 90 minutes. There's little to do in the tiny, affluent fishing community of **Spanish Wells**, and most day trippers watch from the deck of the boat, and get off at exclusive Harbour Island – the only island in the Bahamas that prefers golf-cart traffic and disdains cars and trucks.

Next stop is **Governor's Harbour**, in central Eleuthera *(see page 43)*. If you've only been to New Providence, this is the ideal way to get a feel of the 'Out Islands'. For details, tel: 323-2166 or log onto the company's website: www.bahamasferries.com.

6. Excursion to Exuma

Take a powerboat for a day to a naturalist's dream island. From coral reefs to iguanas, this is a chance to see nature up close.

Just 38 miles (61 km) southwest of Nassau, the **Exumas** make up a 120-mile (193-km) long archipelago. With a base of craggy rock, the beaches are quiet, clean and seldom see what you might call a crowd. And with more than 360 cays, they have the reputation of being the most unspoilt and secluded of all the Bahama Islands.

The Exumas are well known to the sailing set, who cruise there regularly for the annual Family Island Regatta. The closest thing you can find resembling population density is Great Exuma Island, which lies at the furthest end of the Exuma chain, with a total of about 2,000 residents.

Take a 900-horsepower boat from Nassau Harbour to visit these fabulous cays for the day and watch the most exciting spectator sport available – the action happening below the surface. The **Powerboat Excursion** to Exuma leaves from the Captain Nemo Dock (off Bay Street) in downtown Nassau at 9am. Each trip only takes six to eight couples, so it's advisable to make your reservations as soon as you arrive at your hotel (tel: 327-5385).

With a motor four times more powerful than a standard V8, it is not surprising that the boat reaches the Cays in an hour. There are scheduled stops along the way to remind you that there's a whole world under the water you might have forgotten about while you were at the casino. The Exumas are home to the 113,000 sq.-mile (293,000 sq.-km) **Exuma Cays Land and Sea Park**, a protected area that begins north of Staniel Cay. That translates into very few people and plenty of marine life. The waters fairly teem with snapper, grouper, and lobster, and with magical forests of corals.

Join a nature trek

At **Allan's Cay**, one of the few not inhabited by humans, you'll see 3-ft (1-metre) long iguanas wiggling through the bush. The guides relay fascinating information on them, before serving a mid-morning snack of fresh fruit. You'll prob-

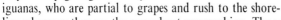

ably end up giving most of yours to the iguanas, who are partial to grapes and rush to the shore-line whenever they see the powerboat approaching. The second stop is made at a spectacular reef in crystal clear water, with many fish and coral formations. Even a timid swimmer will find a shallow swim other-worldly; the underwater shoals are positively stunning.

On the guided nature walk, you'll get a panoramic view of the island and learn some mysteries of the Bahamian bush. You'll see ospreys and egrets – maybe even a wild boar. Halfway along the walk, you will be doused at the freshwater well. It is safe to feed stingrays while you stand ankle-deep in a pool of them. And provided the tide is right, the captain will hand-feed small sharks and barracuda while you stand by and watch.

Lunch is barbecued lemon grouper on the beach at **Ship Channel Cay**. There are free refreshments all day long, from water and juice to wine and local Kalik beer. The beaches are private and the snorkelling spectacular. There's shelter, shade, and a rinse-down shower and toilet facilities.

After lunch, there's further island exploring or, if you prefer more leisurely pursuits after an energetic morning you can simply do some gentle working on your tan for the rest of the afternoon.

By 7pm, the boat is back at the Nassau dock.

Feeding the iguanas

Eleuthera
The Family Islands

There is no public transport on this family of islands – Eleuthera, Harbour Island and Spanish Wells. Visitors make their way by either rental car or with a tour guide. The latter is rare, as most islanders have full-time farming or fishing commitments. Rental cars are accessible but not plentiful, so they should be reserved in advance by your travel agent. Drive on the left-hand side of the road. (As the Bahamian saying goes, 'If you're left, you're right; if you're right, you're wrong.')

Eleuthera got its name from the Greek word meaning 'freedom'. There is only one major paved road here, called the Queen's Highway, so it's practically impossible to get lost. Most side-roads are unmarked, and have always been so. The narrow paths often compete with overgrowth, dirt and loose rock, and only the sturdiest jeeps can brave some of them. However, tucked behind almost every craggy, limestone cliff are smooth, tranquil, pink-sand hideaways well worth seeking out.

Long and narrow in shape, Eleuthera is 110 miles (178 km) of gently rolling hills from end to end, and 2 miles (3 km) across at its widest point. The narrowest part of the island is at the Glass Window Bridge, which is only large enough to permit one car at a time to pass. Some settlements have pay phones, but you can be assured of phone access at every settlement's telecommunications station. The electricity in all areas is quite reliable. The tap water – unlike that of New Providence – is delicious. There are medical clinics in Governor's Harbour, Rock Sound, and Harbour Island, and a nurse's station in the smaller settlements.

Every which way

Hitchhiking short distances is a common practice for both locals and foreigners alike, and is quite safe. On the whole, Family Islanders are extremely sociable; it is rare for them to lock their doors at night, and walking or driving, they are sure to hail friend or newcomer with a wave and a 'Mornin'!'

Preparing lunch

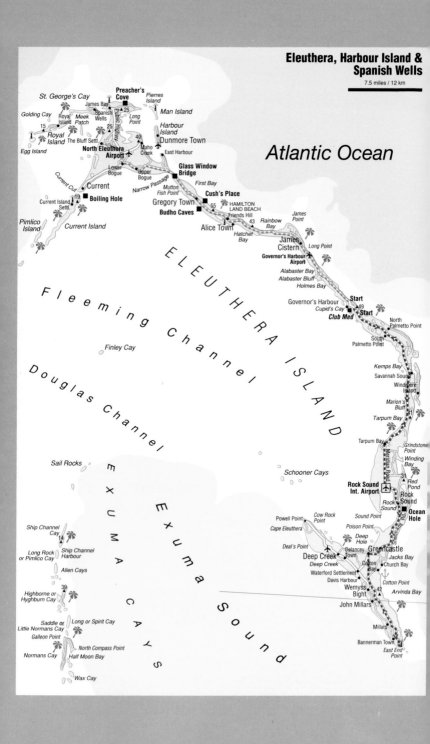

Eleuthera, Harbour Island &
Spanish Wells

7.5 miles / 12 km

Atlantic Ocean

E L E U T H E R A   I S L A N D

F l e e m i n g   C h a n n e l

D o u g l a s   C h a n n e l

E X U M A   C A Y S

E x u m a   S o u n d

Preacher's Cove
Pierres Island
Man Island
St. George's Cay
James Bay
Spanish Wells
Long Point
Golding Cay
Royal Island
Meek Patch
The Bluff Settl
Harbour Island
Dunmore Town
15
25
25
40
Royal Island
Maho Creek
East Harbour
Egg Island
North Eleuthera Airport
Lower Bogue
Upper Bogue
Glass Window Bridge
First Bay
Current
Narrow Passage
Mutton Fish Point
Cush's Place
19
Boiling Hole
Current Island Settl.
Gregory Town
Budho Caves
55
HAMILTON LAND BEACH
Friends Hill
James Point
Pimlico Island
Current Island
Alice Town
Hatchet Bay
43
Rainbow Bay
Long Point
James Cistern
Governor's Harbour Airport
Finley Cay
Alabaster Bay
Alabaster Bluff
Holmes Bay
Governor's Harbour
Cupid's Cay
Start
49
Start
Club Med
North Palmetto Point
South Palmetto Point
Kemps Bay
Savannah Sound
Windmere Island
Schooner Cays
Marion's Bluff
Tarpum Bay
31
Sail Rocks
Tarpum Bay
Grindstone Point
Winding Bay
Ship Channel Cay
14
Long Rock or Pimlico Cay
Ship Channel Harbour
Allen Cays
Schooner Cays
Rock Sound Int. Airport
Red Pond
31
Rock Sound
Rock Sound
Ocean Hole
Highborne or Hyghburn Cay
39
Powell Point
Cape Eleuthera
Deal's Point
Cow Rock Point
Poison Point
Deep Hole
Sound Point
Saddle or Little Normans Cay
Long or Spirit Cay
Galleon Point
Deep Creek
Deep Creek
Delancey Town
Waterford Settlement
Greencastle
Jacks Bay
Church Bay
Normans Cay
North Compass Point
Half Moon Bay
Davis Harbour
Cotton Bay
Cotton Point
Wemyss Bight
42
Arvinda Bay
Wax Cay
John Millars
Millars
Bannerman Town
East End Point

7. South Eleuthera

This excursion visits settlements in Central and South Eleuthera. The island's main airport is near Governor's Harbour, the second-largest settlement on Eleuthera, and is half-an-hour's flying time away from Nassau. Visitors would do well to pick up a rental car at the airport on arrival, as other forms of transport are very limited.

From the airport exit, turn right on to the island's only major highway, Queen's Highway, which traverses the island from north to south. To start the day, you will travel south, to **Governor's Harbour** itself. I recommend that you return here to stay the night; see the end of this itinerary for details about accommodation.

'The Harbour', as it's called by the locals, has grown up around the picture-postcard **Cupid's Cay**. The colonial influence is still very strong here, as you'll see from the exquisite Victorian architecture displayed in well-maintained homes. These houses could easily belong to the early 19th century, if they didn't seem in such good condition.

The 276-room **Club Méditerranée** site is just around the corner and up the hill from the Harbour's one and only traffic light. Closed

View of Cupid's Cay

in 1999, the resort is due to reopen in autumn 2002. The charming 19-room **Cigatoo Resort**, at the top of Haynes Avenue, is within walking distance of the beach, and employs an Italian master chef.

Next, it's down the Queen's Highway, for a tour of the south. The road passes through Palmetto Point, and a few miles further on, Savannah Sound. In the neighbourhood is **Club Eleuthera**, an Italian-owned, smaller version of the French Club Mediterranée. It has a mostly Italian clientele and a very European atmosphere.

There's a real castle, owned by artist MacMillan Hughes, on top of the hill as you pass through the next settlement of **Tarpum Bay**. One of the prettiest settlements, it has a growing artists' colony. Paradise Sam Productions, on the bayfront, has hand-painted T-shirts designed by a resident artist, Dorman Stubbs, and the Mal Flanders Studio specialises in inexpensive local scenes painted on driftwood. After Hurricane Andrew cut a swath through the island in the summer of 1992, Mal Flanders fashioned a Columbus scene out of the

Colour counts in Tarpum Bay

St Columba's church, Rock Sound

remains of the trunks of two coconut palms, and had the resulting artwork installed in the yard between his home and his studio. For very local nightlife, how could you resist a club here that's called The Dark End Of The Street?

A few miles further along is **Rock Sound**, the largest settlement, which has an airport, and operates the main power station for the island. Get one of the local people to point you in the direction of Nellie Lowe's Haven Restaurant and Pastry Shop. Nellie will fortify you with some decadent homemade pastries and cool refreshments. Grandma's Goodies, a shop nearby, sells great ice-cream if that's your preference.

Five hundred yards/metres further, on the right-hand side of the road, is the **Ocean Hole**. If you have any to spare, you could share some of your ice-cream or pastry crumbs with the grouper and snapper fish that congregate at this pool, which is over 200 ft (60 metres) deep. The fish feed regularly on snacks thrown by visitors.

Continue along the highway, past Green Castle and Wemyss Bight, to **Davis Harbour** – a tiny marina where the island branches in two directions. If you turn right you can drive to **Deep Creek** and **Cape Eleuthera**, where a multi-million dollar resort is due to be completed in 2002.

If you turn left, less than 20 miles (30 km) away is **Bannerman Town**, at the southernmost end of the island. Man-made **Princess Cay** has a sprawling

Weaving straw

beach to accommodate cruise-ship passengers who are shuttled by boat to shore. At the dock is a mini-market that sells straw-work and junkanoo craft.

Now that you've seen the south I suggest that you return to the centre and Governor's Harbour – a straight drive of about an hour. Here I would recommend staying in the beautifully landscaped **Laughing Bird Apartments**, located near the centre of the settlement. In nearby Tarpum Bay is the **Unique Village**, with rooms and villas styled in white wicker and wood, and **Hilton's Haven**, located off the Tarpum Bay beach, for those on a budget.

In the evening you can shoot a game of billiards in the **Blue Room**, and eat a traditional chicken snack while you're serenaded by the old-fashioned jukebox. For something a little glitzier you could get seats for the Vegas-type show at Club Med, if it is open. Or try **Ronnie's Hideaway**, on Cupid's Cay, just over the little bridge at Governor's Harbour. It's the popular local disco, with a live band every weekend. The country's biggest bands always have this club on their itinerary when they are on national tours.

The Eleuthera Ministry of Tourism representative has an office in Governor's Harbour, in the same building as the local post office. It will be well worth your while to take a few minutes to drop in for a chat; they are always friendly and helpful and will let you know about all the local events and festivals taking place during your stay on the island.

8. North Eleuthera

This is a driving tour from Central to North Eleuthera, visiting various sites, from underground caves to pineapple plantations. It includes a visit to the Glass Window Bridge and viewing constellations by moonlight. See map on page 44.

Check out of your Governor's Harbour hotel, because you'll be moving to the northern end of the island today. A downturn in the economy towards the end of the 20th century changed the fortunes of many of the small bars and pool halls that dotted the roadsides of this slender, peaceful island. The hurricanes of 1992 and 1999 took their toll too. Even so, the hardy residents continue to bring warmth to a visitor's experience, be it at a settlement's grocery store, the local fishing hole, or the

Leaving Governor's Harbour

main church hall every Sunday. To miss the island experience is to miss the true beauty of the Bahamian people. The four airports on Eleuthera are evidence that the island's friendliness is contagious.

Hatchet Bay Caves

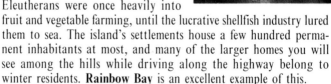

As you travel north on the Queen's Highway, away from Governor's Harbour, you will pass through **James Cistern**, locally known as the 'Speed Bump Settlement', because there are 10 bumps in a row. Pull out your camera now, because the **Cliffs**, just outside this settlement, provide a beautiful photo opportunity.

From one settlement's outskirts to the next, this is all open farm acreage. Eleutherans were once heavily into fruit and vegetable farming, until the lucrative shellfish industry lured them to sea. The island's settlements house a few hundred permanent inhabitants at most, and many of the larger homes you will see among the hills while driving along the highway belong to winter residents. **Rainbow Bay** is an excellent example of this.

About 10 minutes' drive away is the sign welcoming you to **Hatchet Bay**. Its busy, well protected harbour attracts numerous people from the sailing set, and it also serves as a port for the government mailboat, which drops off passengers and supplies twice a week. After the sign, and just beyond the basketball court bordering the Queen's Highway on the left-hand side of the road, is the turn-off to both the dock and the tiny settlement of **Alice Town**.

The **Hatchet Bay Caves** are about 3 miles (5 km) further along the highway. Inhabited by hundreds of leaf-nosed bats, they are a naturalist's dream. If you're interested in exploring them, you can arrange for a local guide to take you through the cave system. (You will need to organise this while you're in Hatchet Bay.)

You'll also need to ask directions to **Surfers' Beach**. About 3 miles (5 km) past the caves, this beach is on the right, about a quarter-mile (½-km) walk away from the highway, along somewhat rocky tyre treads. Park the car by the side of the road, and make the short hike. After walking for 15 minutes or so, across what seems to be nothing but bush, a breathtaking expanse of beach appears over the crest of a small hill.

Experts declare that this is among the top 10 best surfing beaches in the world, and very few people would argue with them. Even if you don't

Surfers' Beach

indulge in the sport, you will find the majesty of those cresting waves awe-inspiring.

Seven miles (12 km) further, past grain silos and open fields, is **Gregory Town**. Its 500 residents deserve their reputation for making it the friendliest settlement in the country. On the right-hand side of the highway, just before the final hill that leads into the settlement, is **Cush's Place**, the ideal spot for a cool drink and perhaps a friendly game of pool with local customers.

I recommend that you stay here, ideally at the reasonably priced **Cambridge Villas** *(see Accommodation, page 85)*. Once you've checked in, go straight to the restaurant and order their extraordinary conch chowder, which is served with decadently delicious home-made bread. The portions are big here, and when it comes to taste, the meals are definitely worth the wait. You may be surprised, if you order a hamburger in this far-flung location, to find it turns out to be the biggest, beefiest, and juiciest burger you have tasted in a long time. They also serve first-rate fish-burgers, made with fish straight from the day's catch.

This region is pineapple country, with around 100 tons a year shipped to local markets in Freeport and Nassau. In 1844, Eleuthera sent its first shipment of these exotic fruits to England. Eleutherans will tell you that it was pineapple seeds gathered from the fields of Gregory Town that were first planted in Hawaii. The rest, shall we say, is history.

Great gifts in Gregory Town

Stop in at the **grocery store**, and get some gas if you need it. You may also want to buy some of the world-famous Thompson Brothers' pineapple rum to take home. It's made from a closely guarded Gregory Town family recipe. Place your request at the store.

Ask anyone in Gregory Town for directions to the **Thompson Bakery**. At the top of the hill overlooking the settlement, the Thompson sisters have a little shop at the back of their home that specialises in mouth-watering pineapple treats. Sample their pineapple or coconut tarts. Their additive-free raisin bread is sold out daily so it's best to get some in the morning, while stocks last. This bread is the kind you will want to eat by the handful, breaking off big chunks, without using butter or spreads. What the shop lacks in frills, it more than makes up for in personalised service.

Before you move on, visit the **Island Made Gift Shop**. Everything here is, as it says, locally made, from jams to T-shirts and jewellery. And while you are here, get instructions about the turn-off to Gaulding Cay, your next stop.

Glass Window Bridge

Two miles (3 km) past Gregory Town, take the turn-off at the left-hand side of the road. **Gaulding Cay Beach** is an exquisite little stretch of sand, no more than a few hundred yards/metres long, tucked away at the end of the path. The water is shallow enough to wade out almost a ¼ mile (½ km) before it reaches hip level. And this in calm, emerald water so transparent that you can see the white sand of the sea floor and every little fish that moves.

Brush the sand from your toes, return to your car and move on to the most breathtaking natural spot on the island, which is just a few miles away. Park at the side of the road, and walk up onto the **Glass Window Bridge**. It's not really made of glass, of course, and neither does it have a window, but it is an actual bridge, just the width of one car, which joins two pieces of the island at the narrowest point. Far below, on one side of the bridge, are the crashing, dark-blue waves of the Atlantic, while on the other side, the emerald-green sea is glassy-smooth, which is how the bridge got its name.

About 15 minutes' drive away are **Upper** and **Lower Bogue**. Have a meal of minced lobster at the **Seven Seas Restaurant** before you cruise back to Gregory Town. Or, depending on the time you arrive, you might want to go to Lower Bogue's **Purple May Club**, which has a live band every weekend.

The most enduring memory you can take back with you from Eleuthera is one that comes free of charge almost any evening: the beautifully clear sky. These islands have few cars and even less industry to cause pollution, so the orange glow that obscures the stars in the industrialised West is absent here. On a clear night the city-dweller may be amazed by the number of stars that are visible, and get an awe-inspiring view of the Milky Way. I have been in Gregory Town during an evening power failure and even with all the street lights extinguished, there was enough starlight for pedestrians to make their way around. So bring along a guidebook to the constellations, and spend an evening gazing at the stars – it's something you will never forget.

A day-excursion on the Bahamas Fast Ferry, headquartered at the Paradise Island Bridge, gets you to Harbour Island on an air-conditioned catamaran, in under two hours. Spend the day here, and be back at your hotel by sunset. See map on page 44.

Harbour Island, just 3 miles (5 km) long and ½ mile (1 km) wide, is five minutes by water taxi off the northern coast of Eleuthera. It is famous for its 3-mile (5-km) wide pink, sand beach – the tiny grains are actually white sand mixed with white coral algae. The quaint architecture is reminiscent of New England, and down-home hospitality exudes from the residents of this former shipbuilding community turned winter resort for the rich and famous. Scooters, bicycles, and golf carts can be hired at several locations, and make a great way to discover the island. Sports fishing and water tours are to be had by the hour or by the half day.

Dunmore Town is to Harbour Island what Nassau is to New Providence: the pulse of the island. It is the home of

Harbour Island view

the oldest Anglican church in the Bahamas, **St John's**, which was built in 1768. You'll walk off the dock almost straight into **The Landing**, a seven-room, colonial-style restaurant that occasionally makes a warm soup from oranges and bananas, and serves it with freshly baked bread. The outdoor section of its elegant dining room is a verandah that literally sits on Bay Street, in the heart of town. It is run by a former Miss Bahamas, and can be your first taste of the quaint cobblestone culture of this tiny island. The cluster of immaculately preserved, wooden, lattice-work cottages, and over a dozen resorts, make Harbour Island one of the Bahamas' most popular destinations. The exclusive **Pink Sands Resort**, for example, is usually 100 percent full in high season, their 'low' is around 80 percent.

The island has a dozen or more excellent gift shops and galleries. On the harbourfront is the **Sugar Mill**, which has a good selection of ceramics, pottery, jewellery, straw-work, and T-shirts. **Flo's Pastries**, on Clarence Street, sells delicious fresh brown, banana nut, coconut, raisin, and corn breads. **Angela's Starfish Restaurant** at the top of the hill has a panoramic view over the island, and **Sea Grapes Nightclub** is home to recording artists the Funk Gang, who return regularly to perform when not on tour.

Atlantic spadefish

Typical clapboard home in Spanish Wells

10. Spanish Wells

A day's visit to the crawfish capital of the Bahamas to discover rustic charm in a fisherman's hideaway. See map on page 44.

Five minutes by water taxi to the northwest of Eleuthera is **Spanish Wells**, the crawfish capital of the Bahamas (crawfish are Bahamian spiny lobster). The Spanish discovered that the water from this island's wells was the sweetest they had ever tasted.

Most young men here leave school to enter the lucrative, spiny lobster fishing business. They can earn tens of thousands of dollars during the seven-month season, catching lobster and storing them in freezers aboard a Bahamian 'smack'. Per capita, this is the richest community in the Bahamas.

The clapboard houses found in Spanish Wells bear a strong resemblance to those in New England fishing villages, and the lilt in pronunciation harks back to the British accent of centuries ago. Distinctive, too, is the blond-haired, blue-eyed physical presence of these white Bahamians.

There are no cars for hire, though you can get bicycles. Sport-fishing guides will take you around Royal and Russell islands, and the **Spanish Wells Yacht Haven** has dive facilities. Or get yourself a paddleboat and take your time discovering your own island secrets.

Check out the tiny **Quilt Shop** in downtown Spanish Wells, where prices for these works of art range from $285 to $325. The **Spanish Wells Museum** opened in 1991. Inside are artefacts dating back to Columbus's arrival in 1492, and relics from the Puritan Eleutheran Adventurers of 1648.

Afterwards, drop into the **Langousta** for an island lunch made from the day's fresh catch, and hear local people tell the latest fishy stories.

Take a water-taxi

Grand Bahama

Only 65 miles (105 km) off the coast of Florida, towards the northern end of the Bahamas lies Grand Bahama. The island takes its name from the Spanish *gran bajamar* (great shallows). One of the last of the islands in the Bahama chain to be settled, it became permanently inhabited in the early 19th century.

The easy money to be made from blockade-running during the American Civil War caused an abrupt exodus in 1861. Only when industrialist Wallace Groves created the design for a planned 'second city' at a clearing in a pine forest near Hawksbill Creek was the island rejuvenated and its full potential realised.

Groves signed a lease – called the Hawksbill

On the edge: West End, Grand Bahama

Creek Agreement – in 1955, for 50,000 acres (20,00 ha) of land, promising in exchange to construct a deepwater harbour. He would pay for all government personnel employed in this free port area (which gave the capital its name), and reimburse the government for all other services.

And Grand Bahama has never looked back. In contrast to Nassau, the wide, clean streets of Freeport are uncluttered by traffic or litter. Water, electricity, telephones and television services are well maintained, and residents of the Freeport/Lucaya area in particular are sophisticated in both dress and lifestyle. With few local bars or corner shops, the physical layout of the island's urban centre discourages beggars or loafers.

Bahamasair has six flights daily to Nassau, and two each day to South Florida. Although you have to commute by cab or bus from the airport, once you get downtown, local buses, charging $1.50 per passenger, run the length of the island until sunset. Taxi tours are available and are recommended, as this is one of the Bahamas' largest islands. You can also rent cars, at about $75 per day, bicycles at around $10–$15 per day and scooters, at $35 per day *(see Practical Information, page 83, for details)*.

11. Freeport – Lucaya

A visit to the town's casinos, nature gardens, the International Bazaar, Port Lucaya and the attractions to the east side of Freeport. You could finish this long day with a romantic dinner at Pier One.

I've started this itinerary from the airport on the basis that most people will be flying to the island and hiring a car. However, if you are already staying in downtown Freeport, you can easily pick up the route from breakfast at Mr Baker's.

Rand Nature Centre

Coming from the **Grand Bahama International Airport** your first exit will be at a roundabout called Independence Circle. Remember always to keep to your left when driving. You will then be on a short strip of road called the Mall. A left turn at the gas station would take you onto East Settler's Way, and towards the **Rand Nature Centre**, home of the Bahamas National Trust. The centre has nature trails and a low-key Bahamian guide who explains the flora and fauna of the island.

But you are going to keep on the main road for now. Past the Civic Centre there are three Canadian-owned banks on the right-hand side of the road, with the main **Post Office** just visible behind the Royal Bank. (Canadian banks hold 80 percent of all deposits in the Bahamas.)

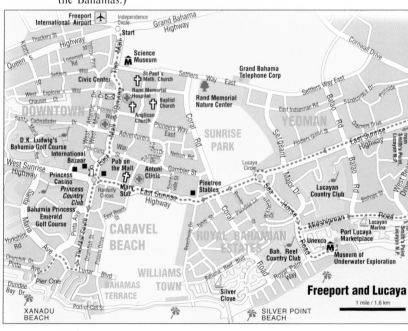

Freeport and Lucaya

1 mile / 1.6 km

The next set of traffic lights marks the intersection with Pioneer's Way, the centre of the city section. On the left, in a pink, colonial building, is the Grand Bahama Port Authority Headquarters. Assuming you've arrived first thing in the morning, grab a quick breakfast at **Mr Baker's**, which is just across the road from Wendy's on East Mall Drive. Ask them to prepare you a little packed lunch to eat later on.

Hair care at the Bazaar

A mile or so further down the road – you're still on East Mall Drive – is Ranfurly Circus, named after a popular British colonial governor of the 1950s. It is the home of the famous **International Bazaar**, a collection of more than 90 shops, lounges, and restaurants with products and architecture representing almost 30 countries.

At the entrance to the bazaar is a bright red, 35-ft (10-metre) high *torii*, the Japanese traditional gate of welcome. Pop into **Silvano's Café** for some homemade ice cream and *spumone* to enjoy with your Italian cappuccino or espresso (tel: 352-5108). Across the street is the **Pub on the Mall**, which offers a typically English meal of bangers and mash (sausages and mashed potatoes) and a pint of English ale.

If you continue across the roundabout and along the Mall South, you will reach the 965-room **Bahamia** resort. The resort has a man-made pool and a beach, literally dug from a part of the highway. In addition Bahamia manages the **Ruby Golf Course**, and a large casino (tel: 350-7000). Also on the complex is the John B, an open-air dining room and bar.

In the distance you can see the refinery and a deepwater harbour. On the channel entrance to that harbour is **Pier One**, built on stilts over the water like a New England fish warehouse. You can watch the ships dock from here. Continuing straight down the mall, you'll get your first good view of the ocean.

Off Pier One is the **Xanadu Beach Resort**. Millionaire recluse Howard Hughes lived here for a number of years, on its 12th and 13th floors, until his death in 1976. The Xanadu has a marina and there is another – called the Running Mon – nearby.

But now we shall go back to Ranfurly Circus, and turn right along the East Sunrise Highway. You will pass the Pub on the

Upcoming attractions

SIR WINSTON CHURCHILL PUB

HAPPY HOUR
5 - 7pm WEEKDAYS

MON *Ladies Night* 3rd CHAMPAGNE 9th

TUES **ENGLISH NIGHT**
DARTS Tournament ENGLISH LAGER BEER

WED The **GONG SHOW** Live ENTERTAINMENT

Golden-Oldie

FRI & SAT Live Entertainment

SUN Calypso Music & Bahamian Limbo Contest

The 'Dolphin Experience', UNEXSO

Mall, Pinetree Stables (where you can ride on horseback trails both inland and on the beach), the Sunrise Shopping Centre (which stays open after the downtown supermarkets are closed) and the Freeport High School.

Another mile (2 km) along, just after the Coral Road intersection, you'll arrive at the **Lucaya Circle**. The second exit around the circle takes you on to Sea Horse Road, which leads to the **Lucayan Beach** – the location of all the major hotels on the island.

The **Port Lucaya Marketplace** opened officially in 1989. With 85 Art Deco-style shops and ongoing open-air entertainment at the bandstand in Count Basie Square, it is probably the most popular spot on the island. To the north, across from the hotels, is an extensive, man-made canal system which has several small waterfront hotels and the largest yacht basin on the island: the **Lucayan Marina and Hotel**. Just a stone's throw away there are two more 18-hole golf courses: the Lucaya Golf and Country Club, and the Reef Golf Course, both part of Our Lucaya Resort.

The Lucayan Beach area is where most of the action takes place. In the daytime there are organised boat trips for fishing and snorkelling. Next to Port Lucaya is the **Underwater Explorers Society** (UNEXSO). At UNEXSO, one of the most respected and comprehensive dive centres in the world, you can learn to dive, they promise, in just three hours.

You can also swim with the dolphins at their popular 'Dolphin Experience'. At Sanctuary Bay, which is probably the largest dolphin facility in the world, nine Atlantic bottlenose dolphins swim out to a reef to interact with scuba-divers in 40 ft (12 metres) of water. The less ambitious can mingle with the dolphins in an open water pool. You can parasail, too, or hire a Boston whaler or windsurfer. In the evenings, the **Prop Club** a sports bar at Our Lucaya Resort, across the road from Port Lucaya, gets pretty busy.

Lucayan National Park Beach

Now return to the Lucaya Circle round-about, and continue along the East Sunrise Highway. After about 2 miles (3 km), turn right at Churchill Drive, then left on Midshipman Road. It's time to get your camera ready because you are entering the **Garden of the Groves** – an exquisite 12 acres (5 ha) of botanical gardens only 10 miles (16 km) away from the city centre (about 15 minutes by car). Browse through the straw market at the entrance, and leave time to visit the **Grand Bahama Museum** on the same property, which contains marine life exhibits, an explanation of the African origins of junkanoo (the national festival), junkanoo costumes, and rare Lucayan Amerindian artefacts.

The garden next door has 5,000 varieties of shrubs, trees and flowers. Wander through (and under) the waterfalls and ponds, and enjoy a visual feast for the eye of the exotic and brilliantly coloured tropical plants, which seem to be springing up from everywhere.

From there, drive 15 miles (24 km) further east along Midshipman Road, to the **Lucayan National Park** (tel: 352-5438). Signed trails will lead you through a mangrove swamp, and the **Lucayan Caverns** – the world's largest underwater cave system. The sunlight playing on the water inside the caves is especially beautiful in the cooler, early-morning hours. You can snack on the goodies from your lunch box while you're there.

Then cruise back, along the wide, well-manicured and uncluttered East Sunrise Highway to the city centre. There should still be a few hours left of the day to wander around the shops at either **Port Lucaya** or the **International Bazaar** at Ranfurly Circus (both have tourist information offices). In the latter, take a tour of the **Perfume Factory**, where you can mix, bottle, name and label your own fragrance. Across the street, above Colombian Emeralds International, is another factory where you can watch local craftsmen create jewellery. If you are tired, or don't feel like shopping, you could take a paddleboat ride or a glass-bottomed boat trip around the harbour.

Dine at **Pier One**, on a patio area overlooking the shark show; they'll be fed at the same time as you. At Port Lucaya, there's free entertainment every night. You can stroll past the boardwalk stalls, or enjoy live calypso and fire dancing under the stars.

Dusk falls on Lucayan Beach

12. West Grand Bahama

A tour of the western end of the island, rich in history and folklore, and a chance to perfect your suntan at any one of the beaches scattering the coast. See map on page 59.

A tour of the West End may be the ideal way to take advantage of the Ministry of Tourism's 'People-to-People' programme. Begun in 1975, it has developed a scheme in which more than 1,000 volunteers throughout the country are chosen, on the basis of age, interests, hobbies, and religious affiliations, to assist visitors in feeling 'at home away from home'. They give you a glimpse of Bahamian life as you might see it when visiting a friend – just as we hope this book does. In advance, or even after you've landed on the island, you can call the People-to-People Unit of the Grand Bahama Tourist Office, located in the International Bazaar (tel: 352-8044).

Breakfast at Becky's

Another option, if you'd rather look than drive, is a bus tour from Freeport to Eight Mile Rock and West End. The four-hour tours allow you to stroll through the streets, bargain at the local shops, and sample native dishes in the village restaurants. Check with the Tourist Information Centre or your hotel for more information.

With or without the company of a local resident, you can start the day with some coffee any time after 7am at **Becky's Restaurant** at the corner of East Sunrise Highway and East Beach Drive – that's about ¼ mile (½ km) from the resort at Bahamia, and well worth the trek (tel: 352-5247).

If you're driving, take the West Sunrise Highway to the Queen's Highway. A series of small settlements dots the route towards West End, at the far western tip of the island. Each place is small, with a few nondescript shops or stores, but worth a look to appreciate the contrast between the Port Authority and the rest of the island. You should be careful as you drive through these settlements, however: children play in the road day and night.

Eight Mile Rock, the next settlement, is exactly that – stretching both east and west of the historical Hawksbill Creek. It is the Bahamas' third-largest community after Nassau and Freeport. About 1½ miles (2 km) into the Eight Mile Rock area, stop off and have a full

Rural region

Liquor store, Eight Mile Rock

breakfast at **Triple D Restaurant**. People in this area are very friendly. At **Hanna Hill**, about 1 mile (2 km) away, visitors frequently find themselves engaged in conversation with people from the community; quite often you'll be invited to join them for a chat on their porch.

About ¼ mile (½ km) further along, you can stop for a cool drink at the **Friendship Shopping Centre**. If the water is beginning to look tempting and you've brought along your swimming gear, **Deadman's Reef**, near the small subdivision of Holmes Rock, has good diving off its cays. In a bay protected by the reef is **Paradise Cove**, a small, family-run watersports centre. The Mount Olivet Baptist Church is the only point of interest in the Holmes' Rock and Seagrape area. Almost all the residents of Seagrape are descendants of Turks and Caicos Islanders who first came to the island in the days before Freeport, when the timber business was flourishing.

Just past Bootle Bay is the **Chicken Nest** – a local bar whose regulars will challenge you to a friendly game of pool or backgammon as Rosie, the proprietor, prepares a bowl of fresh conch salad for which people make the 20-mile (30-km) drive from Freeport.

West End, at the western tip of the island, has a main street lined with bars, shops, and houses. It was frequented by rum-runners and Al Capone during the bootlegging days of US Prohibition. There is a service station and a straw market where you can buy

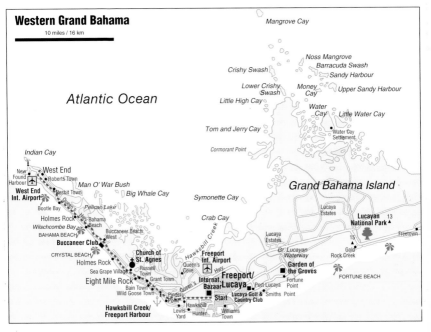

59

Free rein on Russell Town Beach

inexpensive, last-minute souvenirs from this end of the island. Before you leave, pass by **Old Bahama Bay**. On the property is a gorgeous 2-mile (3-km) nature trail, cottage-style suites, swimming pools and a marina, as well as a small gift shop and a bar.

As you retrace your route to Freeport, take note of the turn-off to the right, at the entrance to the **Buccaneer Club**. It's the best restaurant on the island, outside Freeport. Sprawling on to its own ¼-mile (½-km) pristine beach, it offers thatched cabanas on the outside patio, and provides a rustic ambience indoors, with chandeliers and hurricane lamps above its spacious, oak-pannelled dining room. It's the perfect place for your last evening meal on the island, and worth driving back from the city later on.

As you retrace your route, try to find a local person to show you the '**boiling hole**' next to the coastal road along the ocean front of Eight Mile Rock. A boiling hole is an entrance to a subterranean cave system. A bubbling convergence of water creates a vortex in both directions, depending on the tide, and the pressurised water coming out of the hole appears to boil. Just past the Freeport Harbour, at **Pinders Point**, you'll see another boiling hole called 'The Chimney'. This rural area also borders the busy Lucayan Harbour, the destination of a number of major cruise lines.

Russell Town occupies a beautiful stretch of beach south of Freeport, at the southern end of North Beachway Drive, a road much used by equestrians from the **Pinetree Riding Stables**. Take a pleasant trail ride along their beach at this attractively landscaped, secluded spot.

If you are hunting for beaches at the end of the day, there are others I'd recommend: just east of Lucaya, three fine stretches run into one another – Taino Beach, Smith's Point, and Fortune Beach.

The end of another day

They are popular with local people as well as with visitors.

Alternatively, take Midshipman Road past the Garden of the Groves to the **Lucayan National Park**, a 35-minute drive east of Freeport. You can spend a delightful few hours meandering through the honeycombed collection of limestone caves here. Across the road from the cave entrance is a quiet, pristine, white-sand beach. It's the perfect place to take a break and work on your tan.

Then it's back to your hotel, with just enough time to change for dinner. Get a good seat for the casino show at the **Casino at Bahamia** – a tasteful blend of Bahamian and Vegas-style entertainment.

Shopping

If you're interested in the exotic and the exclusive, you've come to the right place. Bay Street, the main street of downtown Nassau, is a shopper's paradise, carrying a 'who's who' of brand names of products from around the world. The same is true for the International Bazaar and the Port Lucaya Marketplace, on Grand Bahama.

The Bahamas government has eliminated the import duty on several international brand names. The Bahamas Duty-Free Promotion Board accredits merchants who give an unconditional guarantee of authenticity to every designer- or brand-name product they carry. Look for the pink flamingo symbol in the window that indicates participating stores.

Don't expect to do much shopping when you get to Eleuthera or the other Out (Family) Islands. Clothing and gift stores are rare, the quality questionable, and the prices inflated. Once you're on any island other than New Providence or Grand Bahama, it's better to invest in the hospitality, good food and clean beaches.

Bahamian-made Androsia fabric is a good buy, as are the locally made perfumes, liquors and liqueurs. Visit the straw markets on

Spoilt for choice

any island, and try bartering with the vendors over the prices of shell-craft, straw-work, and affordable local paintings. Conch, whelk and intricate coral and gold jewellery are also available. While sampling the local rums and liquors, you might want to try the national beer called Kalik.

Leather

Prices for leather goods range from 15 to 40 percent less than in the United States. For everything from bags to shoes, be sure to visit the Brass and Leather Shop on Charlotte Street in Nassau. The Fendi Boutique imports the real thing, direct from Italy. It's at the corner of Bay and Charlotte streets in Nassau. And Gucci, located beside Rawson Square, has an excellent selection with a large range of accessories.

Crystal and China

Little Switzerland on Bay Street, Nassau, carries such lines as Waterford, Swarovski, and Lenox. The Midnight Sun in the International Bazaar in Freeport also has a varied selection, including Baccarat, Daum and Herend.

Cameras

John Bull's Camera Centre offers Nassau's finest display of cameras and other photographic equipment. Nikon, Canon, Vivitar and Olympus cameras and related accessories are on sale at impressively discounted prices. The company has several branches in Nassau, Paradise Island and Freeport.

Lalique glass on Bay Street

Clothing

The pre-shrunk colour-fast cotton fabric known as Androsia is batik-dyed, cut and sewn at the Androsia factory in Fresh Creek, Andros. Motifs such as native fish, shells, flowers and birds are brilliantly displayed in such vivid colours as conch pink, sea green, and aqua-tide. Look for this distinctive fabric at the Mademoiselle shop, on Bay Street in Nassau, and in the Paradise Island Resort and Casino. The pretty **Seagrape Boutique**, on New Providence, also sells a selection of Androsia fashions, as well as handpainted jewellery and T-shirts. The fabric makes a welcome gift or souvenir to take home and it has the advantage of being light to carry and easy to squeeze into a suitcase.

Androsia batik is hard to resist

Watches and Jewellery

The top merchant on Grand Bahama for both jewellery and watches is Colombian Emeralds International, the leading emerald retailer in the world, with major stores in the International Bazaar, Port Lucaya Marketplace, and the resort at Bahamia. Shoppers can make savings over US prices of around 20 to 50 percent.

Colombian Emeralds International also has four stores on downtown Nassau's Bay Street. They feature emeralds, of course, but also diamonds, sapphires and rubies. There are also two outlets on Paradise Island.

Local coral and pearl

Cartier's exclusive boutique on Bay Street carries a wide range of high-quality products. In addition to the renowned 18K gold Cartier jewellery, it sells sunglasses, watches, scarves, money clips and letter openers – all bearing the Cartier name.

John Bull offers a wide array of quality merchandise, from watches and jewellery (Dolphin line, by Kabana, in 14K gold and silver) to perfume and cameras. Their exclusive lines in watches include Rolex, Cartier, Gucci. John Bull also has certified Rolex technicians, and there are branches throughout both Grand Bahama and New Providence.

Galleries

Junkanoo paintings commit to canvas the vivid Caribbean colour box. There is a cluster of galleries situated around Bay Street in Nassau that are excellent sources of genuine local colour. Charlotte's Gallery has a wide selection of paintings by well-established and unknown artists. Marlborough Antiques is co-owned by artist Brent Malone and is a good source of Junkanoo paintings, as well as books, jewellery and, of course, antiques. Best of the Bahamas, near Bay and Parliament streets, also displays and sells a selection of good-quality local arts and crafts.

Perfumes

The Beauty Spot, on Bay Street, offers a complete line of American and French cosmetics, including Elizabeth Arden, Clinique, Estée Lauder, Lancôme, and Chanel.

Freeport's Caribe fragrance factory creates unique fragrances from special formulas, using native flowers like jasmine, frangipani, white ginger, gardenia, and fruits and herbs such as bay rhum, lyme, spyce, and

Works by local artists

Take home the taste of Kalik beer

'mysterious muske'. It also has after-sun moisturisers and an Aloe Vera gel to help maintain a healthy tan. If you take the factory tour (at the International Bazaar, *see page 57*) you can mix, bottle and give a name to your own personal fragrance.

Alcohol

Wholesale Wines and Spirits is on Nassau's Robinson Road, next to the Marathon Mall. Names such as Bailey's Irish Cream and Hennessy Cognac, as well as the domestic brands, are available at prices substantially lower than in the US and Canada. The Crystal Palace Casino in Nassau also has duty-free liquor shops. You can tour the Bacardi Rum Distillery on New Providence and buy bottles of the famous product. If you have room in your hand luggage you could also take home some locally-brewed Kalik beer.

Sweaters and Special Souvenirs

The Nassau Shop has a wall-to-wall selection of fine Irish and British woollen sweaters and scarves. Look for Pringle sweaters and other ready-to-wear fashions. Paperweights, made locally from authentic Bahamian stamps, depict some of the flora and fauna and historical scenes native to the islands. These reasonably- *Mounted coin* priced souvenirs can be found in Nassau at Coin of the Realm, Bernard's and Marlborough Antiques.

The Pipe of Peace, on Nassau's Bay Street, has a fine selection of imported tobaccos, cigars, film and Polaroid cameras.

Coin of the Realm on Charlotte Street has an extensive collection of gold coins from the Bahamas and from all over the world. The company can mount almost any coin and it can be put on a 14K or 18K gold or sterling silver chain.

Eating Out

The variety of Bahamian restaurants is very much geared to the tourist economy. You can get anything from sushi to schnitzel here, not forgetting the staple fast food outlets, but don't pass up the Bahamian home cooking, which can be found in even the most touristy local restaurants.

Prices here are about the same as in any American city – local Bahamian restaurants tend to be cheaper and can range from gourmet to genuine native speciality. A 15 percent tip is considered standard for good service. Most restaurants and bars automatically add it to the bill. Ask if you're not sure.

Stuffed grouper

A traditional Bahamian breakfast is fish stew and johnny cake. The fish is usually freshly caught grouper – a firm, white fish that tastes somewhere between sole and crab. It is boiled, with a few pieces of potato and some onions, salt and peppercorns. The baked johnny cake is really a sweet-tasting cornbread, served hot from the oven. Britain's influence has also put bacon and eggs on most menus, although grits (mashed corn) are easily substituted for the bacon if you don't eat meat.

Conch ('conk') meat, taken from the shellfish of the same name, is the national seafood. Conch salad is usually the raw conch, chopped, with onion, green pepper and fresh tomato, and marinated in lime juice. Variations include baked, fried, or 'steamed' conch – morsels sautéed in a tomato-based sauce, loaded with onions, green peppers and subtle spices. Grouper, snapper and lobster (crayfish) are usually accompanied by brown pigeon peas and rice.

More chicken is eaten than any other meat or seafood, probably because the sea produce fetches a good price when exported. Peas and rice and potato or macaroni salad make up the side dishes.

Desserts may be a huge slab of chocolate cake or hot apple pie. Don't pass up the homemade lemon or lime pie, though; it is made from local fruit, and has just the right sweet-tart taste. For a truly decadent experience, try the guava duff.

In the following listings, meals (excluding alcoholic beverages) costing up to $15 per person are considered to be inexpensive, $15–25 moderate, $25–40 above average, over $40 expensive.

New Providence and Paradise Island

BUENA VISTA

Delancy Street
Tel: 322-2811
Built in the 1800s, this renovated mansion in Nassau's downtown area has Continental and Bahamian selections on its menu, as well as the Vintage Club, with an excellent in-house jazz combo. Open at 6pm, it serves dinner from 7pm. Closed Sunday. Reservations advisable. *Above average.*

Bahamian buffet

CAFÉ JOHNNY CANOE

Next to the Nassau Beach Hotel
West Bay Street
Tel: 327-3373
An unusual, but very pleasant ambience is created by the native wood, photos of old Nassau, and original Bahamian art, at this, one of Nassau's popular restaurants. Located on the Cable Beach strip, it has an excellent breakfast, lunch, and dinner menu. Service is exceptional, and there's live music and a Junkanoo 'rush' every evening. *Moderate.*

CLUB LAND'OR BLUE LAGOON RESTAURANT AND LOUNGE

Paradise Island
Tel: 363-2400/2
See the stars through the stained-glass ceiling. Romantic candlelight, native seafood and international cuisine. Dance to a live band after dinner, served from 5–10pm. *Above average.*

CROCODILES – HOME OF THE LAST QUARTER

East Bay Street
Tel: 325-2148
This is really two restaurants with the same management. Step outside to the deck of Crocodiles, which overlooks Nassau Harbour, and enjoy hearty hamburgers and fries under your own thatched gazebo. There is also live entertainment at the Last Quarter on weekends. Open from 11am, with Happy Hour Monday to Friday from 5–7pm. *Moderate.*

GRAYCLIFF

West Hill Street
Tel: 322-2796
email:bigbite@batelnet.bs
www.graycliff.com
The Bahamas' only 5-star restaurant. From the tuxedoed livery man who opens your car door to the Baccarat crystal and world-famous wine cellar of the 250-year old estate, it's easy to see why it was rated one of the world's top 10 restaurants by *Lifestyles of the Rich and Famous*. Though pricey (about $100 per person), the food, service and ambience are unforgettable. Dinner served from 6pm. *Expensive.*

Graycliff: luxury in a 250-year-old estate

An ocean view at Traveller's Rest

SEASIDE BUFFET
Nassau Marriott Resort
West Bay Street
Tel: 327-6200
In an advantageous location just opposite the casino. There are international and Bahamian selections at the gigantic breakfast, lunch and dinner buffets – complete with a three-tiered dessert section – which make it easily the best bargain on the island for the truly hungry visitor. Open from 7am–4am. Dress is casual. *Moderate to above average.*

CAPRICCIO'S CAFÉ
Cable Beach, corner of West Bay Street and Skyline Drive
Tel: 327-8547
Authentic Italian specialities, ranging from their homemade ice-cream to pasta and desserts. The tiny café has chequered tablecloths, flowers at the table, and cheery service at modest rates. *Moderate.*

TRAVELLER'S REST
West Bay Street
Gambier Village
Tel: 327-7633
I give this place top marks for informal island atmosphere. With the best banana Daiquiri on the island, it has an excellent Bahamian menu to match the ocean view from the patio. Open 11am–11pm. *Moderate.*

Fatman's Nephew

Grand Bahama

BUCCANEER CLUB
Deadman's Reef
Tel: 352-5748
With its own beach, the Buccaneer offers complimentary fritters, reasonable prices, and excellent Swiss-Bahamian cuisine. *Above average.*

MR BAKER
East Mall Drive (opposite Freeport Inn) downtown
Tel: 352-8666
Mr Baker's coffee shop serves tasty Bahamian breakfasts from 7am. Also open for lunch, but the real draw is fresh breads and pastries. *Inexpensive.*

FATMAN'S NEPHEW
Port Lucaya Marketplace
Tel: 373-8520
Grilled fish to order as well as American and Bahamian cuisine. *Moderate.*

FERRY HOUSE RESTAURANT
Pelican Bay, Port Lucaya
Tel: 373-1595
Elegant seafood and gourmet desserts at this intimate patio restaurant overlooking the harbour. *Expensive*

PIER ONE
Freeport Harbour
Tel: 352-6674
Sharks provide the floor show here. Excellent seafood. *Expensive.*

Try for a ringside seat at Pier One Restaurant

PUB ON THE MALL
Opposite International Bazaar, Freeport
Tel: 352-5110
Freeport's oldest and most authentic English-style pub. Also a superb Italian restaurant and a funky grill room and rotisserie. *Moderate.*

TONY MACARONI'S ROAST CONCH EXPERIENCE
Taino Beach, Lucaya
Tel: 375-1652
Roasted conch and other shellfish served from a thatched beach hut several days a week. *Inexpensive.*

Eleuthera

BUCCANEER CLUB
Governor's Harbour, central Eleuthera
Tel: 332-2500
Try their Conch Creole special. They also serve sandwiches and light lunches. (No credit cards.) *Moderate.*

CAMBRIDGE VILLAS
Gregory Town
Tel: 332-0080
Best deal on the island; extraordinary conch chowder served with hot homemade bread. Open for breakfast, lunch and dinner. *Moderate.*

HARBOUR LOUNGE
Harbour Island
Tel: 333-2031
Located by the waterfront, ideal for watching the sun go down, and within walking distance of the straw market. Try the 'five-in-one' soup, or grilled chicken. *Inexpensive.*

MATE AND JENNY'S
Palmetto Point
Tel: 332-2504
Serves lunch and dinner, but worth making the trip just for the delicious homemade pizza. *Inexpensive.*

SEA GRAPE RESTAURANT AND BAR
Spanish Wells
Tel: 333-4371
You can dine either indoors or *al fresco* in the patio bar. The emphasis tends to be on the day's fresh catch of fish, but beef and chicken dishes are also available. *Moderate.*

Pineapple pastries

69

Nightlife

The most readily available entertainment on New Providence and Grand Bahama is to be found in the casinos, of course. Even if you don't think of yourself as the gambling type, you really shouldn't pass up a visit just to experience the electricity in the air as the dice roll and the bets are being made. From the 5-cent, one-armed bandit to the minimum $400-bet at the baccarat table, they all generate great excitement. Besides, where there's a casino, you can be sure there's a disco, casino show, and live band close by.

Bahamians take their culture seriously, and are prolific and professional when it comes to live performances. Check the theatre listings, or ask at the Ministry of Tourism to find out what is happening and where. Entertainment will include not only original plays and musicals, but also amateur and professional dance ensembles. If you can get a ticket, you will be in for world-class performances at very reasonable prices.

The National Centre for the Performing Arts opened in July 2001, a welcome addition to the Nassau cultural scene. Located near the Paradise Island access bridge, the building, a former movie theatre, has a cultural display in its foyer and hosts regular top-class dance and theatrical performances.

The range of evening activities is decidedly smaller in the Out (Family) Islands, where a night on the town will only happen on weekends, and will most likely be at a hotel bar. Fortunately, that's the charm of true island living, and a game of dominoes or billiards at a tiny bar can become a wonderful experience and a lasting memory.

The few discotheques and nightclubs that do exist are those that can count on local people as their regular customers, rather than catering to a fast tourist turnover. What these places lack in glitz and high-tech, they more than make up for in island hospitality.

Nassau Marriott Resort and Crystal Palace Casino

Nassau as night falls

Each of the daily newspapers on New Providence and Grand Bahama has an entertainment section which is regularly updated. The *What's On* magazine (Aberland Publications), overflows with information about nightclubs, discos, evening sports competitions, and concert, theatre and cabaret venues. It includes most of the Out Island nightspots, too.

Whichever island you visit try not to miss the lively fish fry. This is usually a weekly event, where local people and visitors dance and eat tasty Bahamian cuisine washed down with a Kalik beer. Taino Beach is the place to be, in Grand Bahama on Wednesday evening. In Nassau there is a popular fish fry at Arawak Cay.

There is a Ministry of Tourism Office on every island; the representatives are knowledgeable and friendly, and will often go the extra mile to ensure your needs are met.

Bars

John B Bar
Freeport
The Resort at Bahamia
An informal open-air dining room and bar with a DJ, open on selected days. Patronized by resort guests and local people looking for a relaxed evening.

RUBY SWISS
Freeport
adjacent to the Resort at Bahamia
There's a relaxed drinking atmosphere at the bar and the dining area has good live music in the evening. Ruby Swiss is great for real night owls: open 11am–6am.

Jazz

THE VINTAGE CLUB
Delancy Street
Buena Vista Restaurant
Nassau
Tel: 322-2811
A contemporary jazz combo performs in a genuine bistro atmosphere. The bar opens at 6pm.

Live Calypso

BLUE MARLIN 'NATIVE' EXPERIENCE
Blue Marlin Restaurant
Hurricane Hole Shopping Plaza
Paradise Island
Tel: 363-2660
Steel pan music and limbo dancing are laid on for your after-dinner entertainment.

Cocktail time

groups. There are bars in the square and the atmosphere is always vibrant.

Cabaret/Revues

CASINO ROYALE ROOM
Resort at Bahamia
Freeport
Tel: 352-7811
This is a two-hour cabaret show, featuring French cancan dancing.

THE PALM COURT LOUNGE
The British Colonial Hilton
Bay Street
Nassau
Tel: 322-3301
Veteran recording artist Jay Mitchell, backed by the Fine Tone Trio performs calypso and reggae favourites.

Nightclubs

AMNESIA
East Mall Drive
Freeport
Tel: 351-CLUB (2582)
A club with a state-of-the-art sound and light system. Caters to teens and 20-somethings.

BAHAMA BOOM BEACH CLUB
Elizabeth Avenue, two blocks east of
Rawson Square
Nassau
Tel: 325-5907
This club is just a few minutes' walk from the cruise ship dock in downtown Nassau and has a great dance floor and laser shows accompanying a different theme every night. Open from 8pm until very, very late.

CAMBRIDGE VILLAS
Gregory Town
Eleuthera
Tel: 332-0080
As well as having a good restaurant, this popular hotel has disco weekends, from Thursday to Sunday evening. Local people come from all over the

CLUB 601
East Bay Street
Nassau
Tel: 322-3041
Two live bands perform alternate sets at this club from 7pm.

CROCODILES – HOME OF THE LAST QUARTER
East Bay Street
Nassau
Tel: 325-2148
There is a live calypso band at the Last Quarter every Friday and Saturday evening.

PORT LUCAYA MARKETPLACE
Lucaya
Grand Bahama
Tel: 373-8446
There's free live entertainment at the bandstand in Count Basie Square on the waterfront from 8pm to midnight. During the week there is calypso and *soca*, and on Sunday during the late afternoon there are gospel performances by local and international

island to show off the latest dance steps in their glad rags. Dress casual and be prepared to dance until dawn.

CLUB 601
East Bay Street
Nassau
Tel: 322-3041
With a live band playing every night and a wild happy hour on Friday, when local recording artists, Visage, are featured. This place is very popular with a more mature clientele (i.e. the baby boomer generation). Open Thursday to Sunday.

CLUB WATERLOO
East Bay Street
east of Paradise Island Bridge, Nassau
Tel: 393-7324
Five bars and live music on weekends, at Nassau's largest indoor/outdoor nightclub.

THE ZOO
West Bay Street
Saunders Beach, Nassau
Tel: 322-7195
This is Nassau's largest club, and current favourite. Two storeys tall with no less than six bars. Open 8pm–4am.

Theatres

DUNDAS CENTRE FOR THE PERFORMING ARTS
Mackey Street
Nassau
Tel: 393-3728
Comparable in quality to Broadway, but set in a more intimate venue. Call to find out what's in repertory.

REGENCY THEATRE
Freeport
Grand Bahama
Tel: 352-5533
'Friends of the Arts' put on original plays, and sponsor guest performers from abroad.

Cruises

BAHAMA MAMA CRUISES
Port Lucaya Marketplace
Grand Bahama
Tel: 373-7863
Enjoy a sunset catamaran cruise, which includes a meal and live entertainment. Numbers are limited so be sure to

Boogying Bahamian style

book. There is also a two-hour 'booze cruise' that includes unlimited rum punch and snacks. Cruises begin at 6 or 6.30pm depending on the season.

EVENING DINNER CRUISE
Calypso I and Calypso II
Paradise Island Terminal
Paradise Island
Tel: 363-3577
Hop on board one of the two *Calypso* boats and take a cruise to the secluded Blue Lagoon Island for a romantic, three-hour dinner while afloat. Fittingly, there is calypso entertainment performed by a live band. Cruises are from 7–10pm and reservations are advisable.

SUNSET CRUISE
Flying Cloud
Paradise Island Terminal
Tel: 363-4430
Watch the sun set and see Nassau Harbour and Paradise Island by night.

Calendar of Special Events

New Year's Day, a public holiday, truly begins at 4am in Nassau, Freeport and on almost all the Out Islands. In the open-air Junkanoo Competition, groups dressed in elaborate and colourful costumes of crêpe paper vie for cash awards and instant fame as they 'rush' down the main streets dancing to the infectious rhythms of cowbells, goatskin drums, whistles, and a variety of homemade instruments. Many Bahamians belong to Junkanoo groups sponsored by local businesses *(see also June celebrations, page 76)*.

Court opening

The Bahamas Windsurfing finals are held, culminating at the Lucayan Beach Hotel, Freeport.

The Changing of the Guard ceremony in Nassau takes place every second Saturday of the month in the grounds of Government House, at 10am. This time-honoured tradition of pomp and pageantry marks the changing of the guard of the Royal Bahamas Police at Government House, the official residence, since 1801, of the Governor-General, who is the Bahamian representative of Queen Elizabeth II.

The Supreme Court Opening, Nassau. This picturesque ceremony opens the first quarterly session of the Bahamas Supreme Court. The Chief Justice, dressed in ceremonial robes, inspects a Royal Bahamas Police Force Guard of Honour in front of the Supreme Court building. The internationally famous Police Force Band performs throughout the year.

The People-to-People Tea Party is held in Government House Ballroom, 4–5pm, on the last Friday of each month. A full British tea is served to the first 200 guests, with the wife of the Governor-General in attendance.

The Bahamas National Trust Annual Open House, held at the principal agency of environmental preservation in the Bahamas, Nassau. Performances by an 'environmental' actor, garden

Junkanoo drummer

The police force band in action

tours, and a showcase of indigenous snakes and birds are some of the varied highlights.

FEBRUARY / MARCH

The Archives Annual Exhibition, focusing on the history of the Southern Bahamas, is held in the foyer of the main Post Office Building, Nassau.

Annual Grand Bahama 5000 (5K) Road Race. Billed as the number one race of its kind in the Caribbean, it features world-class athletes, top local runners and walkers, and offshore participants. It has a grand opening, featuring bands, cheerleaders, bed races, and a children's fun run.

APRIL / MAY / JUNE

Annual International Dog Show and Obedience Trials, in Nassau. Categories include hounds, sporting dogs, toy terriers, working, non-sporting, and special 'pot cake' (mixed breeds) class. Entries from abroad are welcome.

Supreme Court Opening *(see listing for January)*.

The Bahamas National Amateur Golf Championship is held in Lucaya, Grand Bahama. Amateurs from all of the Out Islands compete, with the winner gaining automatic membership of the Caribbean Amateur Championship team.

Labour Day, on the first Monday in June, is a public holiday.

The Eleuthera Pineapple Festival, Gregory Town, Eleuthera. Held in June, it celebrates the world's sweetest pineapples, grown on plantations throughout the island. There is a junkanoo parade, a pineapple recipe competition, various craft displays, the plaiting of the 'maypole', and a 'pineathelon' – a swimming, running, and cycling contest that draws an international field of competitors.

Tour de Freeport, a 100-mile (160-km) bicycle race, in Freeport.

Junkanoo in June – celebrations held every weekend of the month, at Arawak Cay, Nassau. Food stalls, artisanal work, and cultural presentations culminate with a Junkanoo 'rush out' by thousands of brightly costumed dancers and musicians.

JULY / AUGUST

Supreme Court Opening *(see listing for January)*.

Independence Week celebrates the independence of the Commonwealth of the Bahamas, with a range of festivities, parades, and celebrations. On 10 July, the national holiday, at West End in Freeport there is a Junkanoo parade, which starts at 4am.

Emancipation Day is the first Monday in August, a national holiday that celebrates the abolition of slavery in 1834. The annual Fox Hill Festival, in Nassau, celebrates Emancipation over a 10-day period with a series of events including an early-morning Junkanoo rush out by the Fox Hill Congos.

SEPTEMBER / OCTOBER

Michael Jordan Celebrity Invitational golf tournament, in September, Ocean Club Golf Course, Paradise Island.

National Heroes Day in October, honours Bahamians who have made a significant national contribution. This public holiday replaces Discovery Day, commemorating Columbus's arrival.

Also in October is the annual conch-cracking competition in McLeans Town, on the eastern end of Grand Bahama.

NOVEMBER / DECEMBER

Father and Son Challenge, at Ocean Club Golf Course, Paradise Island.

Central Bank Art Exhibition and Competition. A national competition

A dab hand at artwork

of young artists (under 26 years) showcasing paintings and drawings in a variety of media.

A Christmas Music Evening is held at Atlantis, Paradise Island, in December. Features choirs, chorales, and the Royal Bahamas Police Force Band.

Annual Renaissance Singers concert. An evening of classical, modern, and ethnic Christmas music held at the Government House ballroom.

The Junior Junkanoo Parade, a competitive display of indigenous Junkanoo music, dance, and festive costumes by primary and secondary school students, is a prelude to the Boxing Day and New Year's Day Junkanoo parades held in Nassau.

Christmas and Boxing Day, public holidays. Starting at 1am the national cultural extravaganza – Junkanoo – takes place in Nassau, Freeport, and most of the Out Islands. Rivalling Mardi Gras and Carnival in colours, sights, and sounds, it has to be experienced, rather than explained. Winners are announced at 8am.

On the green

Practical Information

GETTING THERE

The air travel market is fiercely competitive in the Caribbean region. Fortunately, this pays big dividends to the tourist in the form of great package deals. Check with your travel agent for the best seasonal offers. Nassau International Airport on New Providence is the hub for the area, with Freeport on Grand Bahama a close second. You can get to almost any island from either of these two.

By Air

Eleuthera and the surrounding cays are served by three airports: one at North Eleuthera, one at Governor's Harbour in the centre of the island, and one to the south at Rock Sound. Regular service is available from Miami on Airways International and American Eagle. Flights from Fort Lauderdale are provided by Airways International, Island Express, and US Air Express, while Bahamasair serves Eleuthera from Nassau.

Grand Bahama International Airport is the world's largest privately owned international airport. It has US pre-clearance facilities, and customs and immigration services 24 hours, seven days a week. There are flights from Freeport to Fort Lauderdale, Miami, Nassau, Montreal, Toronto and London in the UK.

Nassau International Airport is the Bahamas' busiest airport. There are frequent daily flights from Nassau to the US, Canada, the UK and the Caribbean.

By Sea

Cruise travel has taken off in the Caribbean, and that includes the Bahamas. International lines dock in downtown Nassau, Freeport and Eleuthera. If you prefer the shorter stays ashore, you might want to try some of the following companies: Royal Caribbean Cruises *(Emerald Seas)*

Prepare for landing

Cruising into port

tel: 800-327-7373; Carnival Cruise Lines *(Carnivale, Mardi Gras, Jubilee, Fantasy)* tel: 800-327-9501; Chandris Cruise Lines *(Galileo, Crown Del Mar)* tel: 800-223-0848; Crown Cruise Lines *(Viking Princess)* tel: 800-841-7447; Premier Cruises *(Dolphin)* tel: 800-222-1003; Norwegian Caribbean Lines *(Sunward, Seaward, Norway)* tel: 800-327-7030; Premier Cruise Lines *(Oceanic, Royale, Atlantik, Majestic)* tel: 800-327-7113; Princess Cruises *(Star Princess)* tel: 800-421-0522; and Royal Caribbean Cruise Lines *(Nordic Prince)* tel: 800-327-6700.

Go ashore by mail boat, that use Potter's Cay in Nassau as the port of entry. These include the *M/V Current Pride*, the *M/V Bahamas Daybreak II*, and the *M/V Harley* and *Charley*.

Bahamas Fast Ferries operates a daily service to Eleuthera, Harbour Island and Spanish Wells, on the *Bo Hengy* catamaran. The first ferry leaves Nassau at 8am and reaches the island cluster in 90 minutes.

Water-taxis to Spanish Wells from the Eleuthera mainland cost approximately $5 per person. From the mainland to Harbour Island costs about $4 per person.

TRAVEL ESSENTIALS

When to Visit

Temperatures are moderate, usually at a low of 60°F (15°C) and a high of 75°F (24°C), almost all year round. The exception are the hot summer months of July and August, when the temperature can range from 80°F (27°C) to the high 90s (around 36°C). In general, the holiday season is year-round, although the slowest time is September/October each year, when many of the attractions and hotels take the opportunity to refurbish.

Visas and Passports

Nationals of the United Kingdom, Commonwealth countries, or EU member states require a passport, but not a visa. US and Canadian citizens must present either a passport or two other forms of identification, one of which must carry a photo, eg. a birth certificate (original or certified copy) and a driving licence. However, a passport is recommended for travel.

Citizens of Cuba, the Dominican Republic and Haiti, and former Communist bloc countries must have passports and visas.

When you travel to the Bahamas from a foreign country you are given an immigration card to fill in. The immigration officer at the point of entry detaches the main part of the card and leaves you with a stub. Be sure to return the stub upon departure. There is a $15 departure tax, with an additional $3 security fee for international departures from Grand Bahama.

Vaccinations

Vaccination certificates are not usually required, unless you have arrived within seven days from one of the following countries: Burkina Faso, Gambia, Ghana, Nigeria, Sudan, Zaire (Congo), Bolivia, Brazil, Colombia or Peru.

Pets

Any pets brought into the islands must be over six months of age and must have a valid import permit. Contact the Director of Agriculture, Department of Agriculture, at PO Box N-3028, Nassau, The Bahamas.

Customs

Residents from the US are allowed duty-free items valued up to $600 retail, provided they are properly declared to the customs inspector. The duty-free exemption can be claimed once every 30 days, provided the resident has been outside the US for at least 48 hours. A family of four may take home $2,400 of duty-free goods. US residents can even take up to $1,000 above the $600 allowance by paying a flat 10 percent duty on the additional purchases. Each resident aged 21 or older can include 2 litres (67.6 oz) of alcoholic beverages if one litre is manufactured in the Bahamas or another Caribbean country. Fifty cigars (not Cuban) and 200

cigarettes can be imported duty-free. There is no age limit on those purchasing cigars and cigarettes.

There is also a flat rate of $1,000 duty for a family of four, which can be grouped to a total $4,000 value for entry at the flat rate of duty; this can be applied no more than once every 30 days.

No tortoiseshell goods, plants, or fruits are allowed.

For Canadian residents, duty-free allowances depend on the time you spend outside Canada, and on previous claims for exemptions. After 48 hours' absence, any number of times a year, you may import up to CAN$200 worth of duty-free merchandise, which must be carried by hand or in your luggage. This may include 50 cigars, 200 cigarettes, 7oz (200g) of tobacco and 60oz (2 litres) of liquor. Once every calendar year, after 7 days' absence or more, you may take home merchandise worth up to CAN$750 duty-free.

Residents of the UK may take back home with them, duty-free, up to 200 cigarettes or 100 cigarillos or 50 cigars or 250 grams of tobacco; 1 litre of alcohol over 33 percent or 2 litres of 22 percent or under; 60ml of perfume or 9 fluid oz of toilet water, up to a value of £145. Check www.bahamas.com if in doubt.

Weather

The Bahamas has its own weather, unlike the rest of the Caribbean. The Gulf Stream bathes the western coast with clear, warm water, and steady trade winds approach the shores from the southwest. The occasional shower is brief and clears quickly. As a result, temperatures seldom drop below 60°F (15°C), or rise above 90° (32° C) except for the odd day or so in July or August.

Take cover at midday
Clothing

A casual spring-summer wardrobe is appropriate for day or evening. You'll probably spend most days in swimwear, shorts, slacks, or jeans. Bathing suits are permitted only on beaches or around pool areas. In the evening, what you wear will depend on your choice of restaurant and after-dinner activities. Semi-formal dresses and suits will suit the mood of the casinos and more elegant restaurants and night spots. Men are expected to wear a jacket and tie after 7pm at most clubs. You may want to bring an extra layer for the cooler winter evenings.

Electricity

Voltage is 120; 60-cycle AC Standard North American shavers, hair dryers, and other appliances can be used. British three-pin plugs will need adaptors, and appliances will need transformers.

Time Differences

The Bahamas operates on Eastern Standard Time (which is five hours behind Greenwich Mean Time) from October to April, then switches back to Daylight Saving Time for the remainder of the year – the same as in cities such as New York and Montréal.

Internet Access

The British Colonial Hilton in Nassau has internet access in every room, charged at 10 cents a minute. There are several internet cafés in downtown Nassau and also in Freeport. Some Out Island hotels also provide guests with access to the internet.

GETTING ACQUAINTED
Geography

The Bahamas is an archipelago encompassing 100,000 sq. miles (260, 000 sq. km), with a land area of 5,382 sq. miles (14,000 sq km). It comprises somes 700 coral-based islands plus more than 2,000 cays and rock formations. Thirty of the islands are inhabited. Technically, the Bahamas is not part of the Caribbean (as is frequently thought), but is in the Atlantic Ocean, and is bordered on the west by the Gulf Stream.

Government and Economy

The Commonwealth of the Bahamas achieved independence on 10 July 1973. Along the lines of the British system of government, the Bahamas has a Prime Minister, although the 49-member House of Assembly (Lower House), and the 16-member Senate (Upper House) have more in common with the US system. Elections must be called every five years. There is also a Governor-General, who is appointed as the official representative of the Queen.

Tourism is the Bahamas' leading industry, employing almost three-quarters of the population and providing close to two-thirds of the government revenue. International banking is the second-biggest industry. There is no income tax; local revenue comes chiefly from import duties and annual business licence fees. Thanks to these tax breaks, foreign investment on the islands is extensive.

Religion

Although the Anglican Church (Church of England) is the official church of the Bahamas, religion has a strong ecumenical history, which means faiths from Ba'hai to Catholicism, Greek Orthodox to Muslim, are well represented.

Safety Precautions

As with all densely populated urban centres, it is wise for travellers to be cautious with personal belongings. If you are staying at a hotel, keep your passport and excess cash somewhere secure, such as your hotel safe. It's not a bad idea to carry a photocopy of your passport with you, in case the original is lost or stolen. In Nassau and Freeport especially you will notice a marked decrease in the number of pedestrians on the streets after sunset, particularly in the downtown areas where there are few places to visit after the stores have closed, other than restaurants. You should keep to the main streets, malls and nightclubs after dark — unless, of course, there is one of the Bahamas' many street festivals taking place. These events are well lit and well policed and it would be a great shame to miss them.

'Down-home' and sincere neighbourliness are still the trademarks of Eleuthera and other Out Islands' hospitality. Day or night, you can feel secure when walking about. Some hotels and guest houses do not even have keys for their rooms!

Population

New Providence, although one of the smaller islands of the Bahamas, is the home of the nation's capital of Nassau and holds 65 percent of the total population, with Grand Bahama and its 'second city' of Freeport claiming 15 percent. The remaining Bahamian population is spread throughout the Out Islands, with the largest concentrations in Eleuthera, Long Island and the Abacos.

'Black' in the Bahamas can mean anything from very dark to quite fair-skinned, as some 85 percent of the population are of mixed African descent; 12 percent are white Bahamians, and roughly 3 percent are Asian or Hispanic.

MONEY MATTERS

In New Providence and Eleuthera, banks are open Monday to Thursday from 9.30am to 3pm and from 9.30am to 5pm on Friday. Freeport banking hours are 9am to 1pm, Monday to Thursday; 9am to 1pm and 3 to 5pm on Friday.

Currency

The only legal tender is the Bahamian dollar (B$), which is easily interchanged with the US dollar, with which it is pegged. Banks and hotels can exchange other currencies at prevailing rates.

Bahamian paper money runs in half-dollar, $1, $3, $5, $10, $20, $50 and $100 bills. (See if you can get hold of the less-common $3 bill or the scallop-edged 10-cent piece — they make great souvenirs of your stay.)

Please note that more than

Martin church, Eight Mile Rock

$10,000 in US or foreign coin, currency, traveller's cheques, etc. imported into the United States must be reported to customs.

Credit Cards and Cash Machines

Major credit cards (Visa, American Express, MasterCard) are accepted at most stores and hotels, although you should bring cash or traveller's cheques to the Out Islands.

There are automatic teller machines (ATMs) on both New Providence and Grand Bahama but they will sometimes accept only Bahamian-issued bank cards.

Tipping

A 15 percent gratuity is automatically added in most restaurants and bars. Nevertheless, waiters and waitresses, as well as taxi drivers and chambermaids, are usually given some kind of tip, and it is much appreciated.

Taxes

There is no sales tax in the Bahamas, but there is a 10 percent tax on hotel rooms in Nassau and Freeport. In the Out Islands, 10 percent is added if a hotel is a member of the Out Island Association, and 5 percent if it is not. There is a $7 ticket tax on the price of each airline or cruise-ship ticket bought in the Bahamas. This is included in the price of your ticket, and should not be confused with the $15 departure tax *(see page 79)*.

Money Changers

Banks are the only means by which you can change currency. They have money-changing branches at airports and ship terminals that operate during regular banking hours only. Some hotels may change limited amounts of foreign currency, but at a hefty commission. It is much more convenient to come to the Bahamas with American dollars in cash and/or in traveller's cheques.

GETTING AROUND

Taxis

On New Providence and Grand Bahama, the maximum taxi fares are set by the government and all taxis are required to have meters in good working condition. For one or two passengers, the first quarter mile costs $3. For each additional quarter mile, add 50 cents. For each additional passenger, you pay an extra $2. There is no charge for accompanied children under three years of age.

Taxis can be hired for sightseeing tours at around $20–$25 per hour, depending on the size of the cab. There is an additional charge for waiting time, at 30 cents per minute. There is no charge for up to two pieces of hand luggage, plus small bags and packages carried by passengers themselves. Each additional piece of luggage costs 30 cents.

On Eleuthera, as on the other Out Islands, distances between airports and accommodations vary considerably, and most cabs do not use meters. Make sure you get an idea of the price range for transportation to and from the airport when making hotel reservations. For example, a taxi from Governor's Harbour to

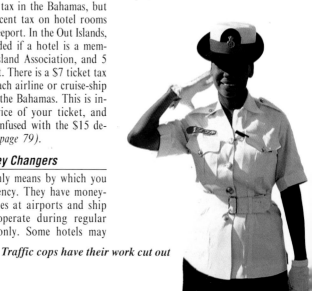

Cambridge Villas, in Gregory Town, is approximately $37.50 for two. It costs approximately $20 for two to get from the same airport to the Laughing Bird Apartments in Governor's Harbour, and $23.25 for two to the Rainbow Inn, in Rainbow Bay. Taxi tours are also a great way to sightsee on Eleuthera, and can be arranged by your hotel or guest house.

Choose your transport

Scooters

These are available for hire at hotels and in downtown Freeport, Grand Bahama at about $35 for a day, or $20 for a half day. In Nassau, New Providence, the prices are higher – around $50 a day. They can also be hired on Eleuthera, though they are harder to come by. A deposit is required, plus $5 for insurance. Helmets are compulsory for both driver and passenger, and swift fines are imposed for those not wearing them. Some places also rent out bicycles; charges are about $25 a day in Nassau, and $10 a day in Grand Bahama, plus a $10 deposit. Whatever transport you have, don't forget to keep to the left-hand side of the road.

Car Rental

Because of the high import taxes in the Bahamas, the rental costs may be higher than you're accustomed to – $75 a day or more. The traffic congestion in New Providence, paired with driving on the left-hand side of the road, if you are not used to it, can make the experience pretty daunting. On such a small island there's really no need for a hired car, especially when there are so many excellent bus services and tours available.

On Grand Bahama and Eleuthera, however, having your own vehicle is the best way to capture the flavour and diversity of the islands in the time you have. In Grand Bahama's Freeport, try Avis on tel: 352-7666, as well as at the airport (tel: 352-7675). Grand Bahama has a well planned highway system around Freeport and Lucaya, traffic jams are virtually unknown.

On Eleuthera the airport taxi drivers, local filling stations, and sometimes private individuals will have cars for hire, as will some local hotels. If you want to have your own transport, ensure you have ar-ranged the rental before you reach the island. Cars can be hired on a daily basis or by the week. Be sure to bring along a valid driver's licence.

Bus Services

The bus service in New Providence covers virtually the entire island. From dawn to dusk, and at a dollar a ride (no transfers), it is a great way to experience the local culture while seeing the sights.

In Grand Bahama, mini-buses leave from the International Bazaar for Lucaya and downtown Freeport. The other type of buses, called jitneys, even though they are public transport, are owned by individual entrepreneurs, so you may find yourself sitting for a while waiting for the driver to get a full load.

To make sure the bus is going where you want to go, ask the driver before you get on. Jitneys run from downtown Freeport to Eight Mile Rock, West End and East End. Check with the Tourist Information Centre or your hotel for more information. A complimentary bus service is provided to the beach by city hotels and by outlying hotels to Freeport.

There are no public buses on Eleuthera, though hotels provide shuttle services to the local beaches and the closest settlements.

HOURS AND HOLIDAYS

Business Hours

Stores are open from 9.30am to 5.30pm Monday to Saturday. The larger malls on New Providence and Grand Bahama are open until 8 or 9pm on weekends, and on Sunday afternoons.

Public Holidays

The following are public holidays throughout the Bahamas: New Year's Day, Good Friday, Easter Sunday and Monday (variable dates); Labour Day, the first Monday in June; Whit Monday (late May); Independence Day (10 July); Emancipation Day (first Monday in August); 12 October is National Heroes Day; Christmas Day (25 December) and Boxing Day (26 December). Most stores are closed on these holidays and on Sunday, except for pharmacies; food stores are open 7–10am only.

Market Days

The straw, fruit, and fishing markets are open daily, and on most holidays as well.

ACCOMMODATION

There are 63 hotels with 8,262 rooms in Nassau/Paradise Island, and 25 on Grand Bahama with a total of 2,818 rooms. During the high season (December to April), a two-bedroomed furnished suite rents from $265–$550 per day on Paradise Island, and at about $200 per day in Nassau. A double room is around $140 a day in Nassau and $180 a day on Paradise Island. On the Out Islands, double rooms cost about $65 per day at the smaller hotels in high season, while the larger hotels charge about $90 per day. For more details check the Ministry of Tourism's website: www.bahamas.com.

Package deals from Miami can slash those rates dramatically, offering three nights, two days for as little as $200 per person. Last-minute package deals from the UK and Europe are also worth shopping around for.

A choice between the Modified American Plan (room, breakfast, and dinner) and the European Plan (room only) is available at most hotels. There is a room occupancy tax of 10 percent (4 percent which is levied by the government and 6 percent is for hotels to fund promotions and advertising).

In the list of recommended hotels that follows, the inexpensive price category means less than $80 per night for a single room. Moderate prices range between about $80–$130 per night and the expensive range is from $130–$170. Luxury accommodation is plentiful throughout the islands, and starts from around $170 per night.

A kidney-shaped pool

Hotels

New Providence

ATLANTIS
Paradise Island
Tel: 363-3000
Website: www.atlantis.com
A luxurious mega-resort that is home to the world's largest man-made marine habitat. With a casino, 11 swimming areas, dozens of restaurants and lounges. *Expensive*

BRITISH COLONIAL HILTON
Bay Street, Nassau
Tel: 322-3301
Website: www.colonialnassau.com
The only hotel in downtown Nassau with its own private beach. Comfortable accommodation and excellent location within walking distance of most downtown shops. *Luxury*

DILLET'S GUEST HOUSE
Chippingham, Nassau
Tel: 325-1133
Website: www.islandease.com
A family home in an attractive Bahamian mansion. It has only seven rooms, and the operators, descendants of the original owners, have produced a real winner. Bed and Breakfast accommodation and good food. Try their delicious homemade chocolate cake and lemonade. *Expensive*

NASSAU MARRIOTT RESORT AND CRYSTAL PALACE CASINO
Cable Beach, Nassau
Tel: 327-6200
The largest resort in the Bahamas, this one has 867 guest rooms, 23 deluxe theme suites and seven other suites. The casino has a choice of several restaurants, a Las Vegas-style dinner club, shops, and a health club. *Luxury*

CLUB LAND'OR
Paradise Island
On the Paradise Island Lagoon
Tel: 326-2400
With 72 rooms and apartments, the Club

Paradise Beach

Land'Or features its own disco, native show, swimming pool and bar with jazz combo. Its Blue Lagoon restaurant serves excellent seafood, among other dishes, under an attractive, domed, stained-glass roof. The complex offers babysitting facilities, too. *Moderate.*

TOWNE HOTEL
George Street, Nassau
Tel: 322-8450
One block from Bay Street and the Straw Market, the Towne has satellite television, dining-room, bar, sun deck, swimming pool. Good rates. *Inexpensive.*

Grand Bahama

BELL CHANNEL CLUB
Located off Jolly Roger Drive in Lucaya
Tel: 373-2673 or 373-3801
This is an exclusive private community offering luxuriously furnished, two-bedroomed townhouses and one- or three-bedroomed beach villas. Special features include private patio porches, ocean and

channel views, central air-conditioning, designer interiors, cable television, whirlpools, and washers and dryers. A security gate is manned 24 hours. There is a bus shuttle, a 36-slip marina, thatched beach and barbecue gazebos. *Expensive.*

OUR LUCAYA BEACH AND GOLF RESORT
Royal Palm Way, Lucaya
Tel: 373-1333
Website: www.ourlucaya.com
Grand Bahama's largest mega-resort has its own golden-sand beach, with misting pools, and luxurious, spacious airy suites. Located across the way from the bustling Port Lucaya Marketplace. *Luxury*

PELICAN BAY AT LUCAYA
Royal Palm Way, Lucaya
Tel: 373-9550
Website: www.pelicanbayhotel.com
European-flavoured boutique hotel with access to the Our Lucaya Beach. Also near to the excellent Ferry House restaurant, the best on Grand Bahama. *Luxury*

RUNNING MON MARINA AND RESORT
Located at Kell Court and Knotts Blvd
Tel: 352-6834
Fax: 352-6835
Website: www.running-mon-bahamas.com
Offers 30 rooms with two double-beds, as well as eight deluxe captain's cabins which have king-sized beds. Also available is the more elaborate Admiral's Suite, which features a furnished living room, jacuzzi, kitchenette and dining area. *Moderate to expensive.*

Eleuthera

CAMBRIDGE VILLAS
Gregory Town
Tel: 335-5080
Fax: 335-5308
Cambridge Villas has rooms and apartments, a popular disco and a swimming pool at reasonable rates. Its kitchen also produces what is arguably the best conch chowder on the island. There's also a five-passenger private plane on hand which can be chartered for island-hopping excursions. Rates range from $70–$100 a day. You should add around $40 per day for breakfast and dinner. *Inexpensive to moderate.*

THE LANDING
Bay Street, Harbour Island
Tel: 333-2707
Website: www.harbourislandlanding.com
Stunning hotel minutes from the famous
pink sand beach. Indoor/outdoor patio
dining offers Australian and Bahamian cuisine, in a colonial ambience with unaf-
fected charm. *Luxury*

LAUGHING BIRD APARTMENTS
Birdie Lane, Governor's Harbour
Tel: 332-2012
Overlooking the Cupid's Cay section of
the picture-postcard harbour, the Laughing Bird has fully furnished efficiency
apartments, and is within walking distance
of the harbour shops and supermarkets.
Arrangements can be made for everything
from shelling trips to golf, as well as car
and scooter rentals. Rentals are from $50
(one guest) to $100 (four guests) per night
plus $15 for each additional guest.

HEALTH & EMERGENCIES
Pharmacies
Many drugs bought over the counter in the
Bahamas may not be taken into the US.
Check with US customs (tel: 377-8461)
before purchasing any medicines that you
might wish to take back with you.

Medical Services
First-rate medical care is available from
both public and private facilities in
Freeport-Lucaya, and in Nassau. Between
the private Doctor's Hospital (tel: 322-
8411) and the 24-hour outpatient department at the Princess Margaret Hospital
(tel: 322-2861) in Nassau, most emergen-
cies can be attended to promptly and ef-
ficiently. For a private ambulance with
paramedics, tel: 322-2881. In Freeport, the
Rand Hospital (tel: 352-6735) is fully
equipped with efficient staff and facilities.
On Eleuthera, there are government clinics
in each settlement, staffed with a nurse
and doctor who can provide medical services at minimal fees.

In the event of an emergency that -
requires particularly sophisticated tech-
nology, Air Ambulance Associates (tel:
305-776-6800) and the National Air

A familiar sight for UK visitors

Ambulance (tel: 305-525-5538), based in
Fort Lauderdale, Florida, offer emergency
transportation in medically equipped
aircraft to hospitals in the United States.

COMMUNICATION AND NEWS
Post
Use only Bahamian postage stamps on your
postcards (40 cents) or letters (55 cents).
Stamps are available at the Main Post
Office, at the top of Parliament Street,
the Shirley Street Post Office, and at most
Bay Street pharmacies in Nassau. There are
also post offices at the International Bazaar
in Freeport, other malls in Grand Bahama,
and in every major settlement on the Out
Islands. Post offices are open from 8.30am
to 5.30pm, from Monday to Friday, and
until 12.30pm on Saturday.

Telephone
There is a 25-cent charge for local calls. The
telephones will accept only Bahamian or
American 25-cent pieces. Public phones are
few and far between; use one at your hotel
or ask for the closest BaTelCo (Bahamas
Telecommunications) station. The area code
for the Bahamas is 242. A 24-hour downtown Bahamas Telecommunications office is
located on East Street, in Nassau. Many
public phones accept pre-paid calling cards
which can be purchased at local stores.

Media

There are three daily newspapers on New Providence, published Monday to Saturday – *The Nassau Guardian* and *The Tribune* in the morning and the *Bahama Journal* in the evening. All of them cost 50 cents. Although you can try to get the papers from the newsstand at your hotel, or from a bookstore, they are in fairly limited supply, so it's best to purchase them from the street sellers early in the morning and at around 5pm. In Freeport, the *Freeport News* is published Monday to Friday, and also costs 50 cents.

Each paper has comprehensive listings of entertainments, and they make great souvenirs. *What's On in Nassau* is also a very useful tourist guide.

USEFUL INFORMATION

People with Disabilities

There is a Desk of the Disabled at the Ministry of Social Services (tel: 323-3333). Staff will be most helpful in providing information regarding specialised transport, access ramps, and special events throughout the year.

Maps and Bookshops

Almost all stores in the downtown areas of Freeport and Nassau will have city maps available at the cashier's station, as will the hotels. Also available are *What To Do* and *Best Buys*, which are free pocket shopping guides with maps of the local shops, as well as discount savings coupons for most of the stores advertised in them. They are updated regularly, and are comprehensive and colourful publications that are of great help to visitors.

The Island Shop, which is located in the heart of downtown Nassau, opposite the Straw Market, has the most comprehensive selection of magazines, newspapers, novels, and other reading material, including a wide selection of works by Bahamian writers.

The BAA (Bahamas Anglo-American) Shop, farther down on Bay Street, and Lee's Book Centre, on Parliament Street, are a few of the easy-access, smaller bookstores that offer a diverse selection of local and foreign publications.

Diving

If you are a scuba-diver be sure to bring your certification card with you, as dive operators will not allow you to dive or purchase air fills without it. It's also a good idea to bring along your log book, to document how extensive your diving experience is.

Language

English is spoken, with a touch of British influence in inflection; British-style spelling is officially used. You will also notice a lilt

Enter another world

of Bahamian dialect, influenced by African, Spanish and Amerindian ancestry.

Sport

In the land of endless summer you can be sure that wherever there are a few patches of open ground, there'll be a sports event in progress. Day and evening events are a daily source of entertainment, and are a great way to experience local culture. Although tradition names cricket as the official sport of the Bahamas, the sea remains king, as the numerous yacht and sailing regattas held here attest.

On dry land, basketball rules, though

Beware: golf carts

softball and soccer are becoming increasingly popular. Outside the Bahamas, the toll-free Bahamas Sports Information Centre, tel: (800) 32-SPORT can give up-to-date listings of events. Information can also be had from the Ministry of Youth and Personal Development, tel: (242) 394-0445, or the major sports complex, the Queen Elizabeth Sports Centre (tel: 323-5163).

Useful Telephone Numbers

Grand Bahama
Duty-free information, tel: 394-3575
Ministry of Tourism Information, tel: 302-2000/322-7500 or Hot Line 325-4161
Long-distance operator: 0
People-to-People, tel: 326-5371
Post Office, tel: 322-3025
Time: 917
Weather: 915
Police and/or Fire Emergency: 919

Eleuthera
Governor's Harbour Police, tel: 332-2111
Medical Clinic, tel: 332-201/2774
Harbour Island Police, tel: 333-2111
Medical Clinic, tel: 333-2227
Spanish Wells Police, tel: 333-4030

FURTHER READING

Bahamas Handbook and Businessman's Annual Nassau (Etienne Supuch, Jr, Publications, updated annually).
Modern Bahamian Society by Collinwood and Dodge (eds) (Caribbean books, PO Box H, Parkersberg, IA 50665, USA).
The Bahamas: A Family of Islands by Gail Saunders (Macmillan Caribbean).
Inside Grand Bahama by Dan Buettner (Fair Prospect Press, PO Box 77033, Atlanta, Georgia 3035, USA).
The Ephemeral Islands: A Natural History of the Bahamas by David G Campbell (Macmillan Education, London, 1978).
Insight Guide: Bahamas (Apa Publications, 2002).
Insight Guide: Caribbean (Apa Publications, 2000).
Paradise Island Story by Paul Albury (Macmillan Caribbean).
Nassau Memories by Deby Nash (Nassau: Memories Press, 2000).
An Economic History of the Bahamas by Anthony Thompson (Nassau: Commonwealth Publishers).

Nassau Harbour at Sunset

Index

food 27, 30, 31, 38
Fort Charlotte, New Providence 29
Fort Fincastle, New Providence
  17, 34
Fort Montagu, New Providence 38
Fortune Beach, Grand Bahama 60
Freeport, Grand Bahama 17, 53, 54,
  58, 64, 69, 72, 73, 75, 76, 77
Fresh Creek, Andros 63
fruit 29

G

Gambier Village, Nassau 35
gardens 27, 28, 30
Glass Window Bridge, Eleuthera 49
glass-bottomed boats 26, 39
golf 35, 77
Governor's Harbour, Eleuthera 43,
  45, 46, 69
Grand Bahama Island 11, 17, 53–60,
  62, 64, 68–9, 70, 71, 72, 73,
  76, 77
Gregory Town, Eleuthera 48–9, 69,
  73, 76
Groves, Wallace 17, 53

H, I, J

Harbour Island 43, 51, 69
Hartford, Huntingdon 27, 28
Hatchet Bay, Eleuthera 48
Hawksbill Creek, Grand Bahama 53
Hearst, William Randolph 27
Henry VIII 11
history 10–17
hitchhiking 43
hotels 84–6
Hughes, Howard 55
Hughes, MacMillan 45
Hurricane Andrew 16
Ingraham, Hubert 16
International Bazaar 55, 57
James Cistern, Eleuthera 47
Junkanoo 32, 33, 57, 75, 77

L, M

Leon, Ponce de 11, 17
Lucaya, Grand Bahama 53, 72, 76
Lucayan Beach, Grand Bahama 56
Lucayan Caverns, Grand Bahama 57
Lucayan Amerindians 10, 22, 57
Lucayan National Park, Grand
  Bahama 57, 60
Lyford Cay, New Providence 36
Malone, Brent 32
Mount Pleasant, New Providence 36
museums 22, 23, 32, 52, 57

N, O, P

Nassau, New Providence 12, 15, 16,
  20, 21–4, 28, 29–33, 34, 53, 62,
  63, 64, 65, 71, 72, 73, 75, 76, 77
Nassau Marriott Resort and Crystal
  Palace Casino, Cable Beach 16,
  17, 28, 33, 34, 73
New Providence Island 12, 14, 17,
  20–38, 43, 67–8, 70
nightlife 50, 57, 70–3
Oakes, Sir Harry 15, 17
Out Islands 13, 43, 62, 70, 75
Palmetto Point, Eleuthera 45, 69
Paradise Island 26–8, 63, 64, 65, 67,
  71, 72, 73, 76, 77
Pindling, Sir Lynden 16, 17
pineapples 49
Port Lucaya, Grand Bahama 57

Q, R, S

Rainbow Bay, Eleuthera 48
restaurants 23, 24, 27, 29, 33, 35,
  38, 40, 46, 48, 49, 50, 51, 57, 59,
  60, 66–9
Rock Sound, Eleuthera 43, 46
Royal Island 52
Russell Island 52
Russell Town, Grand Bahama 60

ACKNOWLEDGMENTS

Photography	**Bob Friel** *and*
12t, 13	**Bahamas Historical Society**
11, 12b & 16t	**Bahamas News Bureau**
10, 14	**Balmain Antiques**
15	**Stanley Toogood**
31b	**Dave G. Houser**
Front cover	**Tony Arruza**
Back cover, 31t, 32	**Wolfgang Rössig for APA**
Handwriting	**V Barl**
Cover Design	**Tanvir Virdee**
Cartography	**Berndtson & Berndtson**

INSIGHT
Pocket Guides

The travel guides that replace a tour guide – now better than ever with more listings and a fresh new design

Insight Pocket Guides pioneered a new approach to guidebooks, introducing the concept of the authors as "local hosts" who would provide readers with personal recommendations, just as they would give honest advice to a friend who came to stay. They also included a full-size pull-out map. Now, to cope with the needs of the 21st century, new editions in this growing series are being given a new look to make them more practical to use, and restaurant and hotel listings have been greatly expanded.

☆ INSIGHT GUIDES

The world's largest collection of visual travel guides

Now in association with

Also from Insight Guides...

Insight Guides is the classic series, providing the complete picture with expert and informative text and stunning photography. Each book is an ideal travel planner, a reliable on-the-spot companion – and a superb visual souvenir of a trip. 193 titles.

Insight Maps are designed to complement the guidebooks. They provide full mapping of major destinations, and their laminated finish gives them ease of use and durability. 100 titles.

Insight Compact Guides are handy reference books, modestly priced yet comprehensive. The text, pictures and maps are all cross-referenced, making them ideal books to consult while seeing the sights. 127 titles.

INSIGHT POCKET GUIDE TITLES

Aegean Islands	Canton	Israel	Nepal	Sikkim
Algarve	Cape Town	Istanbul	New Delhi	Singapore
Alsace	Chiang Mai	Jakarta	New Orleans	Southeast England
Amsterdam	Chicago	Jamaica	New York City	Southern Spain
Athens	Corfu	Kathmandu Bikes	New Zealand	Sri Lanka
Atlanta	Corsica	& Hikes	Oslo and Bergen	Stockholm
Bahamas	Costa Blanca	Kenya	Paris	Switzerland
Baja Peninsula	Costa Brava	Kraków	Penang	Sydney
Bali	Costa del Sol	Kuala Lumpur	Perth	Tenerife
Bali Bird Walks	Costa Rica	Lisbon	Phuket	Thailand
Bangkok	Crete	Loire Valley	Prague	Tibet
Barbados	Croatia	London	Provence	Toronto
Barcelona	Denmark	Los Angeles	Puerto Rico	Tunisia
Bavaria	Dubai	Macau	Quebec	Turkish Coast
Beijing	Fiji Islands	Madrid	Rhodes	Tuscany
Berlin	Florence	Malacca	Rome	Venice
Bermuda	Florida	Maldives	Sabah	Vienna
Bhutan	Florida Keys	Mallorca	St. Petersburg	Vietnam
Boston	French Riviera	Malta	San Diego	Yogjakarta
Brisbane & the	(Côte d'Azur)	Manila	San Francisco	Yucatán Peninsula
Gold Coast	Gran Canaria	Melbourne	Sarawak	
British Columbia	Hawaii	Mexico City	Sardinia	
Brittany	Hong Kong	Miami	Scotland	
Brussels	Hungary	Montreal	Seville, Cordoba &	
Budapest	Ibiza	Morocco	Granada	
California,	Ireland	Moscow	Seychelles	
Northern	Ireland's Southwest	Munich	Sicily	

NOTES

NOTES

NOTES